TRAIN THE
TO HE...

TRAIN THE BRAIN
TO HEAR

Understanding and Treating Auditory Processing Disorder, Dyslexia, Dysgraphia, Dyspraxia, Short Term Memory, Executive Function, Comprehension, and ADD/ADHD

Second Edition

Jennifer L. Holland

Universal-Publishers
Boca Raton

Train the Brain to Hear:
Understanding and Treating Auditory Processing Disorder,
Dyslexia, Dysgraphia, Dyspraxia, Short Term Memory,
Executive Function, Comprehension, and ADD/ADHD
(Second Edition)

Universal-Publishers
Boca Raton, Florida • USA
2014

ISBN-10: 1-62734-003-3
ISBN-13: 978-1-62734-003-8

www.universal-publishers.com

Cover design by Shereen Siddiqui

Cover photo @Cutcaster.com/sirylok

Acknowledgements

To all my students whose uniqueness inspired the stories that will help explain learning differences to the people who read this book. And to my kids, Seth, Ben and Teddy whose ears and brains and their mixed up connection made this work necessary and Bailey whose ears and brain work just fine. Thank you also to my husband for his patience on this emotional journey to getting the job done and for telling me to stop being emotional and fix it. Your faith in me means the world.

Table of Contents

Chapter 1

An Introduction to my Passion

In 1996, I became a mother for the first time. My husband and I had co-created the most wonderful, beautiful, creative, genius who was born to any parents ever. At least, like all first time parents, that is what we thought at the time. He grew and amazed his father and me at every milestone by proving to us just how right we were.

By the time Seth was two, I had a few questions. Like, why did I have to get down on his level every time I spoke to him? Why didn't he seem to hear me? And if he was supposed to be 50 words, if I counted moo and bbrrrrrmmmmm for a truck, he was at 48. Was that ok? We went for a hearing test and were told that his hearing was perfect. We went home somewhat mollified, but still with concerns looming. My husbands' sister assured me that he hadn't spoken until late either and neither had her son, who at that time was a very successful college student.

Before we knew it, we had baby number two. Benjamin was a little more demanding, but said his first word at 4 months, literally. His older brother would pop up over the edge of the tub and say 'boo' over and over again to make his little brother laugh. Benjamin started repeating the word himself at four months. His grandparents didn't believe me. So, when we were at the grocery store, Grandma popped up over the edge of the grocery cart and Benjamin promptly said, "BOO!", and laughed. Our second little amazing, bright, beautiful child had been born into the world.

It was around this time that Seth was severely ill. He developed a pneumonia that moved outside his lungs. He was hospitalized twice and had to have surgery to drain a pocket of infection that developed outside his lungs. He had a chest tube for 3 days and major antibiotics for about 2 months for what was termed atypical pneumococcal pneumonia with pleural empyema that required surgical drainage. Seth was rushed to the ER more than a dozen times in a year with temperatures over 106. The highest recorded was 107.3 and I swear he was over 108 once and I was afraid to measure it. Ten months after chest surgery, Seth had his second surgery to remove his tonsils and adenoids. He was 4 years and 4 months old. We ended up discovering a black mold in our house and the entire house had to be remediated.

Once the mold was removed, all of Seth's health problems including frequent nosebleeds, fluid in his ears, runny noses and high fevers stopped immediately. We needed to play catch up with his speech, so he attended speech therapy for 4 months. He was sent for another hearing evaluation, because I still had some concerns about his hearing. We were once again told his hearing was fine.

With a background in education, I just knew something was not right. We were referred to a Children's Hospital in Kansas City for a complete hearing evaluation. We scheduled and went in for that evaluation. Seth was supposed to be in kindergarten, but I was home schooling him, following my instinct that told me something was going on. The audiologist came out and said the same words I had heard twice before, "Good news, Mrs. Holland, his hearing is perfect." This time I started crying and said, "Then why can't he hear me?" This audiologist then said, "I'm not done yet." She sent me on to another facility where Seth was tested for other hearing problems. That was my first introduction to the term auditory processing disorder. Seth heard at about 68% (Figure 1.1) when there was background noise present, which is actually at the low end of the grey area where a diagnosis can be made. However, because of the struggle Seth was exhibiting, and the other test results, he was diagnosed as having auditory processing disorder.

Figure 1.1: Excerpts from Seth's Test Results

<u>SCAN-C</u>
Filtered words subtest (monaural low redundancy stimuli) – 84th percentile. Seth's ability to understand distorted speech is good when listening in quiet.

Auditory-figure ground subtest (speech understanding in noise) – 16th percentile, 1 standard deviation below the mean. Seth has significant difficulty understanding speech in noise.

Competing words subtest (binaural integration task) – 25th percentile. The competing words subtest is a dichotic listening task that assesses binaural integration. Seth's overall score was 1 standard deviation below the mean, but of note is the difference between the right and left ears. There should be no more than a 15 % difference between ears; Seth's ear difference was 24%. Seth shows a left ear weakness.

I was given some papers with recommendations like preferential classroom seating and was told that unfortunately there was not much that could be done for him; he was going to have to learn to cope.

We started Seth in 1st grade that next year, giving his teacher the handouts from the audiology department and hoping for the best. By the time Seth was in second grade, he sat in the back corner of the classroom and cried if someone spoke to him. You see, my perfect, beautiful, smart little boy wanted very much to make the teacher happy. So if the teacher said something like, "There are two brown cows and two white cows in the field. How many cows are there all together?" Seth, being the smart little boy that he was and wanting very much too please and having heard the word cow out of all that, raised his little hand and said something like, "I saw cows yesterday that were black with a white stripe in the middle." Now if that happens one time, it is ignored. But when that happens over and over again to a little guy, the other kids start to laugh. And smart little kids start to feel like maybe they aren't as smart as they thought they were and their little egos are destroyed and they sit in the back corner of classrooms and try to blend into the woodwork rather than be noticed, spoken to, called on or laughed at. And mommies decide they will not accept that this is as good as it can get for their little ones and start to research ways to help.

Benjamin was doing fine at this point. Benjamin has always had an easy smile and a laid back personality. Benjamin sailed through elementary school with us hearing, at every parent teacher conference, how he was loved by teachers and kids alike. I didn't catch on to little clues like "He's a little behind where I would like him to be in reading, so I have been working with him at recess and he is catching up," that I heard just about every year. His third grade teacher even said, "He does so well in class and then bombs the tests. He is smart and I know he knows the material, so I call him up to the desk and go over it and he knows it, so he is fine." His fifth grade teacher was hard on him in math and worked with him for weeks during recess to get him where she thought he should be. During all this, Benjamin was still getting good grades and was loved by all. When Benjamin hit middle school and went from one teacher who knew him extremely well to a different teacher every hour, he went from A's and B's to D's and F's. We began the process of testing him after one teacher noted that she was concerned that he was not performing up to his ability level and seemed easily distracted. He went to an eye doctor, had his hearing checked, had a full physical and even had the lead levels in his blood checked since our home is quite old. Nothing showed up.

Next he began the process of testing through the public schools. Since he was, at that time, attending a private school, he was being tested by people who did not know him. One came out and asked, "Why are we testing him? I am pulling out material I have not used before because his level is so high." When we were called in to review the results, we were told that Benjamin was not eligible for services because he tested on the 8th grade level overall when he was in 6th grade. It was during this session that my educator brain started kicking in and I noticed a few things. The first was that when he had tested in the fall in a classroom setting at the private school, the results showed him to be on grade equivalent of 3.5. (Figure 1.2)

Figure 1.2

DISTRICT WIDE ASSESSMENTS
Ben was given the Stanford Nine Achievement test in 10/09 with the following grade equivalence results:

Total Reading	3.3	Reading vocabulary	4.2	Reading comprehension	3.0
Total Mathematics	**3.8**	Problem solving	3.4	Math procedures	4.6
Language	**3.9**	Language mechanics	3.6	Language composing	7.2
Spelling	**4.6**				
Study Skills	**4.7**				
Science	**2.7**				
Social Science	**5.8**				
Listening	**4.7**				
Using Information	**4.2**				
Thinking Skills	**3.8**				
Basic Battery	**4.2**				
Complete Battery	**4.2**				

In the next chart, you can see the results of one test Ben was given in March of 2010. When he had tested at the public school in a room by himself, he tested on the 8th grade level. The silence and lack of distractions made a 5 grade level difference in his scores. Then I began looking at the results of another test in which his grade equivalent was at 8.1 (Figure 1.3) and noticed that some areas like story recall and story recall delayed that were at less than kindergarten level.

Figure 1.3

Cheryl Helton Special Education Teacher with the following results.

Woodcock Johnson-III					
(norms based on grade equivalence)					
Subtests	*SS*	*GE*	*Clusters*	*SS*	*GE*
Letter Word Identification	111	8.4	Broad Reading	100	6.3
Reading Fluency	101	6.6	Basic Reading Skills	104	7.3
Story Recall	54	<K.0	Reading Comprehension	90	4.5
Understanding Directions	90	3.9	Broad Math	104	7.0
Calculation	104	6.9	Math Calculation Skills	102	6.6
Math Fluency	99	6.1	Math Reasoning	106	7.5
Spelling	107	7.9	Broad Written Language	96	5.6
Writing Fluency	88	4.5	Basic Writing Skills	104	7.1
Passage Comprehension	86	3.5	Written Expression	88	4.5
Applied Problems	105	7.8			
Writing Samples	91	4.4	Oral Language	91	4.6
Story Recall-Delayed	45	<K.0	Oral Expression	86	3.4
Word Attack	98	5.4	Listening Comprehension	98	5.7
Picture Vocabulary	97	5.6			
Oral Comprehension	103	7.5	Academic Skills	110	7.8
Editing	100	6.4	Academic Fluency	94	5.6
Reading Vocabulary	96	5.6	Academic APPS	94	5.2
Quantitative Concepts	105	7.2	Academic Knowledge	86	4.1
Academic Knowledge	86	4.1	Phoneme/Grapheme Know	89	3.5
Spelling of Sounds	69	1.7			
Sound Awareness	105	7.7			
Punctuation & Capitals	87	4.2	Brief Achievement	110	8.1

As you can see, the areas of understanding directions, comprehension, spelling sounds, and phoneme knowledge showed a significant delay as well, especially when compared to the levels he was performing other tasks. At some point, during that meeting, I reached over and smacked my husband and said, "Oh my God! I know what is wrong with Ben. He has it too."

We went on to explain what was going on with Seth and, once we got past that he was not eligible for services, were directed to the Missouri School for the Deaf to be tested. The results showed that Ben hears in the first percentile when compared to other kids his age when there is background noise present. Overall, he hears only 64% in the right ear and 40% in the left ear of what is said in a typical classroom situation. (Figure 1.4)

Figure 1.4: Excerpts from Ben's Auditory Processing Disorder Testing

Competing Sentences Subtest: Short sentences are presented simultaneously to both ears. The student is asked to repeat only the sentence in the right for the first half of the test and then only the sentence in the left for the second half of the subtest—9th **percentile.**
The total of all the subtests shows that Benjamin's performance is in the 1st **percentile** and is considered to be below the normal range.
Speech-in-Noise Test: Single-syllable word recognition lists were used to evaluate understanding in noise. Each ear is tested separately. W-22 words are presented in each ear at 45 dB SL and the speech spectrum noise is presented at 40 dB SL. The test words and the speech noise are presented to the same ear. Benjamin's responses were 64% in the right ear and 40% in the left ear. The results are significant for both ears. Benjamin's ability to understand speech in noise impaired. Speech-in-Noise is a direct measure of a problem commonly seen in
Auditory Figure Ground Subtest: The student repeats single syllable words that are presented amidst a background of multi-talker speech babble. Both the speech stimuli and the noise are presented to the same ear—2nd **percentile.** These results are abnormal when compared to children of the same age who have no auditory processing disorder. Abnormal performance on this test suggests poor ability to understand speech when there are moderate levels of competing speech or noise in the background. In addition, highly reverberant rooms and a distance between the speaker and listener make speech understanding difficult.

Competing Words Subtest: The student repeats single syllable words that are presented simultaneously to both ears. A different word is presented to the left and right ears—1st percentile.

The results from this test are abnormal when compared to children of the same age with normal auditory processing abilities. Abnormal performance on this test suggests a neurologically based auditory processing disorder. In adolescent subjects there may be delay in the maturation of the neurological pathways, or damage to central auditory structures. For those persons cortical plasticity can result in improved listening abilities with appropriate intervention. Research

It was during that summer that we realized two things. 1. My husband did not have severe selective hearing or lack the ability to plan ahead. 2. Our youngest, then 4 years old, showed all the signs of having the same disability his brothers and father have. In that summer, it went from being a symptom left over from health issues early in life, to a wiring difference the boys in my house have inherited from their father and something that I had to find a way to help my family with.

We have a daughter. She is a beautiful happy, blonde haired and blue eyed child. Since neither my husband nor I are blonde, we wonder how we were blessed with this fair haired beauty. She is happy and smart, making the A honor role most of the time. She has the same vertical challenges as her mother, but is a very aggressive basketball player. She is playing the flute and softball and loves life, animals, all things girly and hanging out with her friends. I mention her here, because she does not appear to have any difficulties with the way her brain processes information. I would be quite negligent in not mentioning her though since so much of this book is about the rest of the family.

The baby of our family is Teddy. Teddy is not only our sweetheart, but the sweetheart of everyone who meets him. I have been told it is the big brown puppy dog eyes coupled with his freckles and the fact that we call him Teddy that makes him so endearing to others. Many of the signs were there early, like they were with his oldest brother, but let's face it, he was the 4th. So if he wasn't talking early, we attributed it to the fact that no one let him have a need, every one of us catered to the little guy. If he said things wrong in a cute way, honestly, it was cute and we let it go. Too often, if he didn't answer when I called, I sent a sibling to check. If he didn't answer a question correctly as he ran by, I called him back and told him to listen to Mommy. He answered me, hugged me with those chubby little toddler arms and said, "You are the bestest mommy. I love you" and off he ran.

When he was in pre-k, Teddy had the type of teacher that all of us wish our kids would have for a pre-k teacher. She was kind, loving and supportive and talked very sweetly to the little ones in her care. She spent time getting to know all of them. When it came to parent teacher conferences, she noted that Teddy was one of the first to complete tasks expected of him like identifying all his letters and counting to 100... but that he didn't seem to grasp concepts the first time they were introduced. He always caught on, just not the first time around. (see Figure 1.5)

When Teddy was in kindergarten I observed a PE class. All the little kindergarteners were lined up on either side of the gym with their backs against the padded sides. The PE teacher said, "On your mark! Get set! Go" and all the little kindergarteners left the wall to run across the gym and then Teddy left the wall. I watched this happen several times and then realized that Teddy couldn't hear the teacher. He responded to the other kids running and then he followed suit. I had seen the same thing happen a few weeks earlier at the Valentine's Day party musical chairs game where he was the first one out. He only moved to sit after the other kids did. I don't think he could hear the music stop. Teddy is now 7, and, before this book is published, he will be tested to see what his level of hearing loss is when there is background noise present and what his other areas of difficulty are.

This school year, we are noticing some areas he is struggling. In math, he does not have his facts memorized. He is also complaining about a couple of the other students in class who, he says won't be quiet and keep bothering him. At home, Teddy is always asking for clarification when he hears a conversation and usually fills in the wrong words. His standard response is to say what he heard, listen again to what was said and then say, "ooohhhhh". We are working on the math facts at home on a daily basis and are telling Teddy to think about what he has heard for a minute before he responds to see if he can figure out something that might make sense.

Figure 1.5-Teddy's Pre-K Grade Card Comments

Area: Mathematical Thinking
Teddy is able to count to 20 and beyond independently. He recognizes his numbers to 20 and is now working on numbers to 30. He does very well with the concrete aspects in math, but has difficulty discussing and analyzing information. He often appears confused with what I am asking of him. I restate the question and sometimes need to restate in a different way and show and example in order for him to understand what is being asked of him.

Area: Scientific Thinking
Just like in his math skills, Teddy understands a lot, but is not always able to communicate his thoughts and does not always understand what is being asked of him. If re-stated or re-worded, he can come up with the answers.

Finally, we come to my husband. We now jokingly say that the wiring difference is all his fault. Charles is a very smart man. I call him the font of worthless knowledge. If he gets little factoids into his brain, they are there for good and can be pulled out randomly. Ask him about an article he read on some Civil War battle and he can pull out the information. He can trace the lineage of most major companies from where they started, who merged with whom and what the company is part of today. Charles has an undergraduate degree in Economics and an MBA with an emphasis in Finance.

He is a Business Development Specialist with the University Extension program. Charles helps people figure out their finances and helps them start companies, grow their businesses, rebrand themselves for success and figure out how to best utilize their cash flows to improve their decision making skills. He writes curriculum, holds business classes and works with international trade. Charles is a 4H Leader, a Boy Scout Leader, is involved at church and in our local government.

However, when working on a project, Charles requires two people running back up for him. He will get to the top of a set of scaffolding with only the tool in his hand to do the immediate job, requiring a runner to get each subsequent tool needed. His schedule must be written down or appointments will be forgotten. He hates talking on the phone, often mistakes tones of peoples' voices and is impossible to talk to with the television on. Charles misses turn offs on the highway if he is talking, has poor planning ahead abilities and often swears he has not been informed about things that are happening. Charles is learning, as an adult who has just had a great deal of frustration explained to him through the auditory processing diagnosis of his children, how to cope with the difficulties it presents.

This is my family. Conversations in our home can get interesting, especially with teenagers. My husband will walk into the kitchen and ask Seth a simple question like, "what are you doing?" Seth, who does not often hear tones and innuendos, will respond back negatively with a comment like, "I'm making breakfast, is that a problem?" As the situation quickly escalates, as one quickly can where people are misunderstanding each other, Ben will walk into the kitchen, covering his ears and yell, "Stop yelling! I hate loud noises!" Teddy who has heard the commotion will then run in and start crying because of what is going on. All this happens before I come down the stairs and get into the kitchen to say something like. "You stop! You don't talk to your father that way! You take the volume down! And you quit crying!" Then I look at all of them and say, "We have got to get this figured out because I am not going to be 87 years old and still trying to fix all your conversations!"

Chapter 2:

Neurological Based Learning Disorders

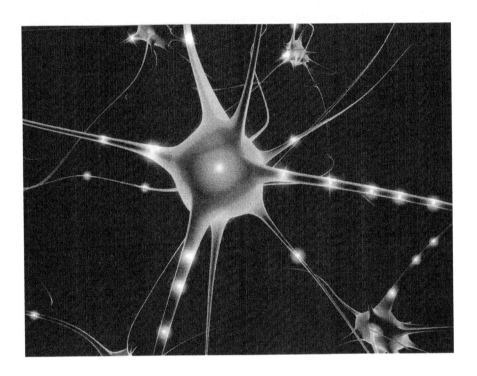

"Everyone is a genius. But if you judge a fish by its ability to climb a tree, will it spend its whole life believing it is stupid?"
-Albert Einstein

Why do I start with this quote? Two reasons: 1. Albert Einstein is absolutely correct- imagine that. 2. Albert Einstein is believed to have some sort of neurological based learning disability. When Einstein was in second grade the teacher told his mother he was unteachable, especially in the area of math and would never amount to much.

**DISCLAIMER: Before I begin, I would like to state that I believe that using 'labels' like dyslexia, dyscalculia, auditory processing etc. do not provide an accurate picture of what is really happening. Using one word to define, not only the difficulty the person has with one senses input, but the specific set of difficulties that the individual is dealing with as a result of that input, undermines that person and often leads to more frustration. It is widely accepted that there is a lot of overlap between the symptoms of the various learning disabilities. I firmly believe that it is better to avoid putting each diagnosis in a convenient box and get to know the individual and treat the symptoms he or she has. Ideally, one should gather information to identify both strengths and weaknesses of each person. That being said, my children and those that I work with have been diagnosed with auditory processing disorder. If I were to label my kids specifically, I would actually say that they are learning disabled. One struggles with auditory and short term memory. One struggles with auditory ,short term memory and prosodic presentation. One of my students has a learning disability that begins with both the auditory and the visual process and includes struggles with comprehension and short term memory. Another of my students has a learning disability that begins with the auditory and the vestibular process and includes prosodic and executive function difficulties. **

What I have found as I work with kids and adults who have these learning disorders is that they are, for the most part, extremely intelligent people whose minds process information differently. If you want to see an impressive "Who's Who" list, do a quick internet search for people with dyslexia; a well known learning disorder. Here are some of the names on that list: George Washington, Walt Disney, Alexander Graham Bell, Henry Ford, George Patton, Leonardo DaVinci, John Lennon, Nolan Ryan, Whoopi Goldberg and Jay Leno. Although not documented, many think that the Wright Brothers also had one of these types of disorders since they were not known to be successful in school, but were able to think outside the box enough to build a plane. NASA often seeks those with these types of disorders

22

since they are known for thinking outside the box. These are bright people whose minds take information in differently. They were born and wired to think outside the box. Because of the way our schools function, they often begin life feeling unsuccessful.

When we discuss learning disorders, we are referring to those disorders that affect the way the brain takes information in, through a system that outwardly appears to work. For example, those who are dyslexic see perfectly, but information, on the way into the brain, gets mixed up. Those who have auditory processing disorders have ears that work perfectly, but on the way into the brain, the signal gets crossed and the information doesn't get there correctly. Dyscalculia is a math based issue. Individuals with dyscalculia often have trouble with math concepts and concepts involving order such as times and dates. Dysgraphia is a person who has difficulty with symbols such as written language, the words may line up correctly but the learner has difficulty making sense of them. These people often have extreme difficulty getting thoughts onto paper, organizing their thoughts and spelling. Dyspraxia is another neurological learning disorder. Those with dyspraxia have difficulty getting body parts to respond the way they want them too. These are people who cannot button their buttons, tie shoes or correctly grip a pencil to perform a task. Someone with dysphasia or aphasia can write down any answer but has a great deal of difficulty verbalizing answers. Often, when they do speak, they are very hard to understand or have trouble organizing their thoughts coherently.

These learning disorders affect learning in one of three ways. The first happens when the **input** is affected. If the input is affected as it is with auditory processing disorders, dyslexia and dyscalculia, the path the information takes into the brain is affected. This is not the same as a sight or vision loss. If the loss is physical, as it is with a hearing loss or loss of vision, the information has no way to get into the brain and the learner and those working with him must find ways to present that information in a way that makes sense for him. We can't give a person who is blind a test on the shades of blue. We can't give a person with a hearing loss a test on identifying the sounds made by the various brass instruments. The information has no way into the brain, no way to be processed and is irrelevant to the learner. Instead, with a learning disability, the path for input remains intact. He can hear and see perfectly, but the path the information travels is affected. To successfully work with the learner, one must find a way to reach, organize and extract that information that was input in a different manner.

Second, a learning disorder can affect the **organization** of the information once it is in the brain. Once we take information in, it must be sequenced, abstracted and organized. Those with learning disorders often have trouble with these areas. The information gets stored randomly so that sequencing is difficult. Many of these individuals find tasks such as telling time, multiplication tables, spelling and months of the year difficult. Once the information has been input into the brain, it must be abstracted so that it fits into a broader picture. A person must be able to understand that they're, their and there are all pronounced the same but have very different meanings and uses. They are taught their times tables and told to do something 3 times. A dog can be a pet and a person who is unattractive is a dog. Then, once the information is sequenced and abstracted, it must be organized. A person who is successful at organizing can put relevant information together, understands and can make good use of time, personal space, calendars and making and following through with plans.

Finally, learning disorders can affect **memory**, which is simply our ability to hold on to and then retrieve information when it is needed. Working memory refers to our ability to hold on to information long enough to make sense of it. To make sense of a sentence, we must hold on to the words until the sentence is complete. To make sense of a paragraph, we must hold on to the information until the sentences are all read. This information is stored in our working memory until we are able to use it.

Those with learning disabilities often have trouble with comprehension tasks, problem solving and math word problems. Our short term memory is often referred to as things we hold on to for 5 minutes or less. It is the list we put in our head as we leave the house. It is the directions a friend gives us to where they are stranded or a phone number. Those who have trouble with short term memory often forget placement of items or conversations, dates and times. Working memory is the mental scratch pad. It is the place you hold onto the running total at the grocery store or where you multiply two digit numbers together. It is the directions you hold onto as you make turns to get to a new place. Once information has passed from short term memory to working memory it is stored in our brain for later retrieval and becomes part of that persons' general knowledge or long term memory. The more we can do for those who have difficulty with working and short term memory at an early age, the more we can do for their overall well being as their long term memory or general knowledge will increase.

Chapter 3:

Auditory Processing Disorders

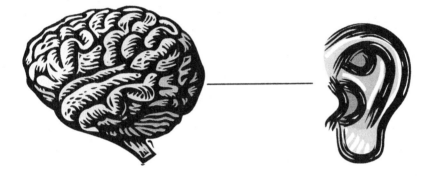

Let's begin with a simple definition. Auditory processing is what the brain does with what the ears hear. When everything works perfectly, we hear everything, whether or not there is background noise present with about 80-90% accuracy. The diagnosis of auditory processing disorder begins when factors, other than a physical hearing loss, cause the person to hear at 65% or less. The area between 65% and 80% is a grey area that indicates a difficulty, but, by itself, is not enough of a loss to be considered a disorder.

To get an idea of what that sounds like, let's begin by doing a little bit of math. Let's start with the fact that the average rate of speech is between 70 and 130 words per minute. So to make numbers easy, we will go with 120 words a minute which is 2 words every second. If the average word has 4 sounds or phonemes, we are being asked to decipher and make sense of 8 sounds or phonemes every second. In the illustration (figure 3.1) for the words black flag, you can see how this might sound to a person who is hearing at 63%, which is at the top end of where a diagnosis of auditory processing disorder starts. In one second, a teacher or speaker will say the words 'black flag' a person with normal range of processing those sounds will hear about 7 of those sounds and easily fill in the one he/she didn't quite get. A person with auditory processing disorders will hear only about 5 of those sounds, loosing an average of 3 sounds and will probably be struggling to put things into context. As you can see from the illustration, the learner will be hearing 'back lg' where the teacher said, 'black flag'.

A learner who is hearing at less than optimal level has the added stress of trying to figure out the information the other learners are trying to absorb that the teacher is trying to teach, but the individual words themselves that are not making sense and they struggle to fill in the blanks and make everything make sense. All the additional background noise gets frustrating as they continue with those struggles. I think of it like trying to pay attention with a mosquito buzzing in your ear. If the mosquito won't go away, your frustration level mounts. For a person with auditory processing disorder, the background noise is like a mosquito buzzing in your ear. You really want it to go away and leave you alone, but it won't. It just keeps coming back again and again, until you can barely stand it.

Figure 3.1

black flag

B-l-a-ck f-l-a-g

b-X-a-ck X-l-X-g

back lg

63%

This is difficult enough to think about one second of the day, now imagine you are 6 years old sitting in a kindergarten classroom and the teacher spends about an hour or two every day talking. How might you react? What will you think of your abilities by the time you are in 4th grade and have been struggling to make sense of lectures and classroom discussions for four or five years?

Let's look at another example. In figure 3.2, we see an example of a 50% hearing loss for the phrase 'green barn'. In this figure, we see the 8 sounds a typical person might speak in a second and what we are being asked to comprehend. Typically a person will hear about 7 of those sounds. In a perfect setting, so will the person with the processing disorder, but when stress or background noise is introduced, the person with the processing disorder will loose about half of those sounds and be trying to make sense of a much different phrase than what was said. Now, put that person with the 50% loss in a high school classroom where lectures are the norm for 4-5 hours a day. After 2-3 hours, is this going to be a person who will be performing to the best of their ability? Will a child with this amount of difficulty still be able to pay attention? Take notes? How is this child feeling about him/her self if they have had a loss like this since they were in kindergarten? How are we, as teachers, professionals or parents treating this child with this behavior?

Figure 3.2

Green barn

g-r-ee-n b-a-r-n

g-X-ee-X X-a-r-X

gee ar

50%

When we begin to answer these questions honestly, we begin to see where auditory processing can cause widespread difficulties in the life of a person who hears this way. Remember, I first noted that it often is found in persons with average to above average intelligence. So these are kids who know when they are little, that they are smart and capable. Then they get to school and they begin to struggle. Teachers say things to parents like, 'he just isn't applying himself' or 'she isn't paying attention in class'. These kids are struggling to complete the work that is expected of them, but lack the ability to tune out the little things around them and are distracted. They may be the kids who are finishing work at recess or at home because it is not getting done in class. As they get older, these are the kids we watch and think, 'he is just not putting out the effort to achieve to his ability level' or 'if only she would apply herself.'

These kids often are also struggling at home and socially. We may even, by middle school, hear the kids say things like they don't have friends or they may become sad, resentful or depressed.

What I tell the kids I am working with is that in a perfect world, someone says something and that information travels straight down the auditory nerve into the brain. The brain synthesizes the information and passes it straight on to where it needs to go. Imagine a fishing line that is pulled tight and that the information is traveling along this line from one end to the other and back. If there is a hearing loss; a physical hearing loss, there is a break in that line. Sounds go in, but there is some reason why it never gets to where it needs to be, the line has been cut. This is not the case for those with an auditory processing disorder. Their line is more like a slinky. The information goes in through the ear, but it loops around in the brain, going from place to place until it gets where it is supposed to be; their processing is slowed down or interrupted. Or, in some cases, especially when the stress level is high or the triggers are strong, the information never makes it where it is supposed to go.

Each person has specific triggers that make this happen. For some, this can happen because there is a lot of background noise and the brain is taking longer to sort out all the information it is receiving. Or if there is a slow down in the processing, the brain may just be taking longer to process what is being said than the speed at which the information is being presented. The other ways in which a processing disorder affects the person happens when stress is high (discussed further later in the book), background noise is overwhelming or there is no past information present in the brain to link the new information too. In these cases, the information is never stored in the brain; it doesn't stick anywhere, and is lost.

Chapter 4

Signs and Symptoms

Now that we now what auditory processing disorder is, we need to know what kinds of things to look for. Let's look at signs for three different age groups of learners: the very young (4.1), preschoolers and early learners (4.2) and school age children (4.3).

Figure 4.1

For the very young:

1. You find yourself physically getting in front of them or on their level to get their attention.

2. The child does not seem to be able to pay attention.

3. Their speech patterns do not seem to progress in a normal pattern.

4. They speak, but are hard to understand.

5. They answer questions inappropriately.

6. The child has a hard time following directions.

As I mentioned earlier, there were things I noticed about Seth when he was just a little guy. He was a complacent, well adjusted child who loved trains and legos, Blue's Clues and Dora and rarely caused us any problems at all. But it was very hard to get his attention. I noticed that I had to get down on his level to get his attention. It wasn't that he was ignoring me or any-thing like that, it just seemed that unless I was squatted down and right in front of his face, he didn't understand me. Being down on his level also insured whether or not he understood what I was saying. Seth could and still can zone out when in-volved in activities. Although he is about 10 inches taller than me now, it is still often difficult to get his attention unless I call his name specifically and he looks at me directly.

Second on the list actually applies more to Ben and Teddy. As young children, neither of them was able to sit and concen-trate on an entire TV show. They would watch for a few minutes and then get involved in a game or other activity. When they were watching TV they would ask so many questions about the story line, that it was distracting to others in the room. Sitting and paying attention to an activity that I wanted them to participate in has always been a battle. Even listening to a story is almost impossible since the line of questions often overwhelms the story line. I would sometimes say things like, 'let mommy read the whole page, then ask questions.' If they pick the activity, they also tend to almost be in their own world, shutting everyone and everything else out.

Third on the list is that their speech patterns do not seem to progress in a normal pattern. For Seth, his number of words and pronunciation were affected. As I mentioned earlier, when he was little, I began keeping lists of the words he said. While he seemed to be a very bright, very perceptive child, he was not talking very much and the words he did say were hard to understand. I also noted that Charles and I still had to interpret everything he said, all the time until he was at least 4 years old. We could understand him, but no one else seemed to be able to. Even though his hearing screenings showed no problems or deficits, his speech was not progressing the way it should be. So at the age of 4, Seth began four months of speech therapy. The problems with his speech were attributed to multiple ear infections and fluid in his ears as a result of allergies.

Next on the list is that they speak, but are often hard to understand. This was the case for our second son, Ben. Ben has what I call hyper hearing. He seems to hear everything everyone says. I now believe this is why he was talking so early. As noted earlier, he said his first word at four months and had several hundred words by the age of two. When Ben spoke, I called his excited speech pattern 'mush mouth.' All his words seemed to run together with no clear beginning or ending. This made his speech seem kind of garbled. When he took his time and slowed down, his words were fine and he was understandable. We took his excited talking as a stage he needed to outgrow and since he had so many words, we were not concerned. As a teenager, he still sometimes has to be told to slow down, especially when he is tired, upset or excited as he still has a tendency in a manner that makes his words slur together and his thoughts to be unclear.

Fifth on the list is one I noticed the most with our youngest, Teddy. Teddy would run by me and I would ask him "Teddy, what are you doing?" Teddy would answer, "Good!" and keep running. I would stop him and tell him to come to me. He would come and I would get at his face level and say, "Listen to Mommy. What are you doing?" He would say, "Oh, playing legos."

Then give me a hug and run off to me saying, "Pay attention to what Mommy is asking." In a home where 4 out of 6 of the people in it often hear the words, but don't hear it right, repeating questions, comments and directions is part of everyday life. Questions that arise because of misinterpretations are amusing. Misunderstandings that happen because of those same misinterpretations can be frustrating, to say the least. With both Seth and Teddy, the need to get down on their level to be understood and the number of times when a question was incorrectly answered was very frequent, especially when they were little.

Finally on this list, we come to having a hard time following directions. By the age of 2, a child should be able to follow 2-3 step directions. A two step direction is; "go to your room (1) get your shoes (2)" or "pick up the toy (1) and give it to me (2). A three step direction is, "go to your room (1) get your shoes (2) and bring them to mommy (3)" or "Go in the kitchen (1), get in the cabinet (2) and get the crackers (3)." Often, a problem in this area is perceived as not listening, or hard headed or forgetful, at least that is what we thought of Ben as doing. I remember telling him to go into the kitchen and get a spoon and bring it to me. He went into the kitchen and turned around, looked at me and said, "Wait, what?" This is normal for Ben. He tries to process what he thinks he has heard, gives it a minute and then asks for clarification.

As Ben got older, we referred to Ben as squirrel because he did this so often. We would say, "Go out to the barn, get in the white cabinet and bring me the hammer." Then 10 minutes later, we had to send someone after Ben, who had made it to the barn and then gotten sidetracked and forgotten what he had been sent for. Kids, who have this type of learning difference, often have short term memory issues. Therefore, they usually remember the first step of a set of directions and then forget everything else. Sometimes, especially when they are small, they will remember only the last direction in a set of directions. This is developmental and normal until the age of about two. So, when given a set of directions, they will look around and try to figure out how to start. For example, if you told your child to 'go to your room, get your shoes and bring them to mommy.' The child might start looking around his feet for his shoes and say, 'where?'

This next section (4.2) deals with kids who are preschool age to early learner age, around the end of first grade. These are the kids who may be entering school for the first time or showing their first signs of struggling, although sometimes the signs may

34

be misinterpreted at this age for ADD/ADHD or other behavioral problems.

Figure 4.2

For the Pre-Schoolers to Early Learners

1. Does not answer questions appropriately.

2. Does not seem to grasp new concepts.

3. Has a hard time paying attention.

4. Seems to always follow, never leads.

5. Still having problems with pronunciation.

6. Phonetic spellings have many errors.

The first sign is that the child does not answer questions appropriately. For and early learner, this might be things like:

> Teacher: What is the next letter after "T" in the alphabet?

> Child: (who wants very much to please and participate and has heard the letter 'T') raises his hand and says 'E comes after T in my name.'

As I mentioned in the first chapter, this can be embarrassing and belittling for a young learner to say the least. More important than that is the damage that can be done to self esteem and self worth. He or she may start to act out, will probably have a hard time concentrating in class when there are a lot of distractions and will have a difficult time completing assigned tasks. These kids are ones who are usually average to above average in intelligence and know that they should know the answers to questions asked. Making it harder is the inconsistencies. Sometimes the learners seem to hear and understand everything and sometimes they seem to miss everything. These are often kids who the teachers suspect of having ADD/ADHD and recommend them for evaluation.

The second sign listed is that the kids often have a hard time grasping new concepts. This seems to be an area Teddy and Ben struggle with. For Teddy, it was first noted in Pre-K when he didn't seem to be able to quickly grasp new concepts. For Ben, it was his teachers in elementary school that noted and helped out every time his ability and his performance didn't match up.

Because new knowledge is acquired by linking it to old knowledge and building on it, new words often make us all stumble. If, however, we are not hearing all the words and phrases, making these connections is often that much more difficult. Young children with processing disorders; whether it is auditory or visual or related to the processing speed, struggle to make sense of every spoken word they hear. When they are introduced to a new word or concept and not given any previous knowledge or links to connect it to, it can be even more difficult to catch on. As mentioned earlier, these kids usually have average to above average intelligence, so the teachers expect them to catch on right away. When they don't, the teacher begins looking for an explanation.

Next is that the child has a hard time paying attention. I am not referring to the child that duct tape would not hold to the seat; that is a behavioral issue. I am referring to the child who appears to be trying to work, but every little thing distracts him/her. I observed two such young learners in a classroom I was substitute teaching in. One child is a beautiful little blond girl. Her hair is always perfectly combed. Her bow matches her outfit and so do her shoes. She sat in class with her unbroken crayons and attempted to do her work. I say attempted because every time ANYTHING happened in the classroom, she heard it and was distracted. A crayon fell on the floor and she got up to help pick it up. A hand was raised, she told the teacher someone needed help. Someone lost part of their work and she went over to try to help. Her work was not being completed because every sound in the room distracted her. On the other side of the room was a very well dressed little boy. He appeared to me to be doing his work until I walked the room to check the kids for comprehension. He had not made a mark on his page past his name. I observed him for a few minutes. I saw that every thing that had the little girl getting up to help; had him loosing his focus. He didn't say anything or do anything; he was just distracted by every little thing that was happening. Often, these are not the kids with behavior challenges. These are the kids whose parents are told things like, 'if he would just apply himself'.

The next thing to watch for is the children who always follow, never lead. In the first chapter, I gave two examples I had witnessed for Teddy involving musical chairs and a PE class. When Seth was younger, I would holler to him to get his attention

36

when he was in a group of kids. I would say his name several times, getting frustrated before I would shake my head as I realized that it was not that my son was ignoring me; he couldn't hear me. I realized that he also could not hear his PE teacher or the conversations in the hall or the teacher on the playground.

Some see these kids struggling and assume it is all part of some bigger picture. After all, these kids don't seem to be getting their work done in class and don't seem to be able to come up with answers quite as quickly as others can and they seem to be the last ones all the time. To many, this is just a sign of a child who is not paying attention or lacks motivation. To the child, this may become a problem as he/she does not understand why he can't ever seem to win. A high energy or competitive child might get frustrated and even act out when this happens time and time again. As parents and educators, we need to pay attention to the frequency of the occurrences and the circumstances when they happen.

The next two signs to look for kind of go together. By the age of 6, most children are speaking very coherently with most of the correct letter sounds in place. A few sounds such as 'th' and 'w' are not expected to be correctly used until the child is school age, but many do use them correctly by this time. If a child has no measurable loss of hearing, but still has many pronunciation difficulties, a processing disorder may be the cause. Often kids who have struggled to hear what is going on around them will make many errors of omission, often at the middle or end of the words. They speak like what they have heard. In the same way the spoken language may have been affected, the written language can show signs of this same problem. Early writers write the sounds in the words that they hear until they have a larger number of memorized words. Therefore, if they have missed hearing a lot of sounds, those sounds will be missing in their written work too.

The last group we will look at in this section is the school age learner and into adulthood. (Figure 4.3) As these difficulties can represent any age learner in school, it is not necessary to further list groups of kids and their possibly difficulties.

First, is that the learner performs poorly on tests. To many of these learners, this is extremely frustrating. Remember, often these are students with average to above average intelligence, so they know the material and they feel they should do as well as their peers on tests. They often prepare for tests as most learners do and feel that they know the material. Then they take the tests and receive very poor grades. This seems to be the case more and more as the students get to middle school and beyond as the responsibility for learning falls more and more on the students. Ben and I had a conversation about this one day. Ben got into the van and threw a test paper in my direction. It

Figure 4.3

School Age Children

1. Child performs poorly on tests.

2. Child does not seem to perform to his/her ability level.

3. Child seems easily distracted.

4. Child has a difficult time with tasks involving language skills.

5. Child has difficulty remembering multi-step directions.

was a test he had prepared for and the grade written on top was a 'D'. Ben looked at me and said, "I don't get it, I knew that stuff." I looked at Ben and said, "I think I know what happens. You get your test and everything is going good. You answer the first five or six questions. Then a kid gets up to ask the teacher a question and you are distracted. Then another kid sharpens his pencil and you are distracted again. Some kid gets up to get a calculator and you are distracted again. Before you know it, someone has finished the test and gets up to turn it in, goes back to her seat, unzips her backpack to put her pencil away, gets into her desk to get out a book. Then several more kids get up and start the same process as they finish their tests. You are still on problem 6, have read it ten times and have no idea what it says." Ben looked at me and said, "You don't even have this problem mom, how do you know?"

Testing frustration can affect the learner in many ways. My son Ben failed his learner's permit test 5 times. My husband finally convinced him to go get some earplugs out of the car and put them in his ears and he was able to concentrate enough to pass on the 6th attempt. He was ready to just give up, having read the book several times and just not being able to get the answers right. These kids often begin to really struggle emotionally as well since they don't understand why they are not successful test takers even though they know the answers.

Often when I go in to start training with kids, this in one of the first hurdles we begin to attack. I tell them that just because they can't take a certain test well does not mean they are not smart. I show them lists of people who had similar problems who are quite smart and very successful and begin to explain.

The second thing listed for school age children is that they do not seem to be performing up to their ability level. Parents are often told, he could get an 'A' if only he would apply himself or if she would just pay attention, she could be getting a much better grade. We are not talking about those kids who cannot sit still or who do not seem to have any self control, we are talking about those who we know are intelligent, but seem to struggle with tasks they should be able to perform. In a classroom, the assumption is that the student needs to apply himself and pay better attention to succeed.

Number 4 on this list is that the child seems to have trouble with tasks that involve language. When people begin to understand auditory processing disorder, they often know that these are kids who are distracted by background noise and so they assume that if the classroom is 'quiet' the students should have no problems. As a matter of fact, the first few times I went in to talk to Seth's teachers, I would explain the problem and get an answer of "He'll be fine. My classroom is quiet." I would furrow my brow and not know what to say next. I have since learned a lot more. My response to that now is, "That is great. So no one ever gets out of their seat with chairs scraping across the floor? No one gets things out of their desks? There is never a lawn mower going by outside? The hallway is quiet? No one asks questions during work time? There is no air conditioner compressor or heating system sounds? The smart board fan is quiet? Most people can tune those sounds out. To my son, that is a rock concert and he can't concentrate on what he is supposed to be doing."

Having said that, please read the next sentence paying attention to what the words are. When you read this sentence can you hear the words in your head? Now think about the words you write down on a piece of paper. Can you hear the words you are writing? We often don't think about all forms of language being disrupted by sounds. The assumption is that the words being spoken by someone else are inundated and confused by other sounds and that is all that is affected. However, when we read to ourselves, we hear the words in our heads. When we write, we hear the words in our heads and the background noise that most of us filter out disrupts all of that language. It becomes harder to read to ourselves and it becomes harder to take notes, as well as to listen. When background noise is present, all forms of language are disrupted.

Finally, we are back to the learner who has trouble with multistep tasks. These difficulties are directly related to struggling with short term memory and can cause serious difficulties in day to day living in and outside the classroom. At home, this is the person who you can give a three step direction and count on having only the first or the last heard and followed. For example, if you tell them 'go in the kitchen and take the hamburger out of the freezer,' they will either look at you and ask "what freezer?" or they will go into the kitchen and come back a minute later with a glass of water, having not completed the assigned task. At school, this is the child who never has all the needed materials.

One of my clients, Rachel, is a girl who probably weighs 90 pounds on a bad day. The first year I worked with her, she was an 8th grade student. She came to her training session at the library twice a week, usually carrying two backpacks with her. One day, Rachel turned around and dropped her backpacks on the table and the sound they made let me know they were heavy. I asked, "What in the world do you have in there?" To which she replied, "All my stuff." I asked what was in her locker and she said, "A mirror and brush and some makeup."

Over the course of the next several sessions, she revealed that there had been too many instances when she had gotten to class, only to realize she had forgotten something in her locker. Whether it was book, notebook or homework; forgetting these items resulted in a loss of points. It just became easier for her to carry all of her things with her, all the time. At the start of the next school year, we tried to set up a color coding system in her locker to alleviate the problem. We tried to set it up so that she knew that the first time she went to her locker, she needed all the stuff in the red box, etc.

It was not long before I noticed that extremely heavy backpack with her again. When asked about it, she explained that she was still forgetting stuff because she didn't always get it into the right place before the school day started. She had also had some difficulty forgetting to bring necessary items home. It was easier to back to have an empty locker and carry all her stuff on her back. This year, Rachel is a sophomore in high school. When asked about her locker this year, she revealed she isn't using it at all. Fortunately, there are several classes that don't even have physical books, so she is not carrying as much as she was a couple years ago.

Another of my students seems to take this difficulty to the extreme. When I first met Cameron, he was a 15 year old high school freshman who had a pass so that he could leave every class early; it is written into his IEP. Cameron had several instances where he went to his locker and, with the hustle and bustle of a large school between classes, froze and could not get his locker open. So, not only was he embarrassed because he could not get his locker open, but he then had to go to his next class unprepared because of it. It got to the point where his fear of not being able to open his locker caused anxiety attacks for him and he became physically ill at the thought of going to school. Now that he has the pass, he has the option to leave class early and avoid the crowds. Because the hallway is overwhelming, he does sometimes find himself in a panic and goes and sits in the school counselors' office until he is prepared to go to the next class.

Many classroom situations also become difficult for learners with these struggles. When the classroom teacher gives directions like, 'get out your math books, turn to page 147 and do numbers 1-23 odd,' these students are the ones who get their math book out and start looking around not knowing what to do next. These are also the students who never know which paragraph they are supposed to read when the class is reading out loud or what they have read once they finish the piece.

The inability to carry out multi-step oral directions is just one part of what makes short term memory difficulties hard. In chapter 12, we will look into short term memory and treating those difficulties in more depth. Difficulty with short term memory also affects those coping skills such as opening your locker and figuring out what supplies to bring to class making it a big concern for the success of a student. The good news is that not only can we work on retraining the brain to more successfully utilize this skill; we can also establish coping methods that will allow them to take matters into their own hands and increase self esteem in the process.

Chapter 5

Types or Presentations of Auditory Processing Disorders

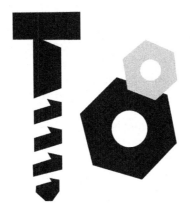

There is not just one defined way that auditory processing disorder presents itself in learners, there are many. Some people have just one main presentation while others have parts of all of them. What I have also found interesting is that it is not always the level at which the loss of hearing occurs that determines the level at which the person is affected. A recent family I began working with has a son who hears at 64% in one ear and 24% in the other. He is reported as being on grade level by his teachers this year, although he struggles with reading and comprehension. Another student I am working with hears at 49% and 68% and is having trouble with all math skills and reading comprehension and is not considered to be on grade level.

The five presentations of auditory processing disorder are: decoding, integration, prosodic, associative and output-organization. Following is an explanation for each of those types.

The first type is called a decoding deficit (fig. 5.1). These are the kids who always turn around and look at you and say, "What?" They struggle to put the information they have received together in a timely manner. If given a passage to read that has new vocabulary, they can read it, but have no idea what they have read because these terms make it hard for them to comprehend. They have the same difficulties when the new vocabulary is spoken. The processing speed at which a learner hears the information causes them to try to quickly make sense of what they have heard. When the vocabulary is new, the task becomes more difficult. Benjamin and Teddy are my kids that have the most difficulty with this. I can watch them try for a second or two to figure something out; then they look at me and say, "What?" As both a mother and a trainer, I wonder how much they miss during the school day.

Often times when people are beginning to understand the concept of auditory processing disorder, they incorrectly assume that the problem can be handled much like that of a person who has experienced a hearing loss. I have had teachers speak loud and slow to my kids thinking that will solve the problem. But auditory processing disorder is not a problem of being unable to hear, but rather more like they hyper-hear. A person with auditory processing disorder does not have the ability to filter out incoming sounds like most of us do. They hear everything, all the time. So when they are involved in something like a group project where there is a classroom full of learners who are bouncing ideas off one another it becomes difficult to focus on the task at hand. Benjamin definitely exemplifies this trait. When he is in situations such as group work, he hears a little bit of what each group is doing. Sometimes, he can tell you what all the projects are for the entire room, but can't tell you what task he needs to complete. Private conversations with a child like this in the house are almost non-existent. He does not have a hearing loss; he hears everything and does not have the ability to filter it all out. I have often wondered what a symphony sounds like to him and others who hear like him.

As mentioned in the chapter pertaining to the symptoms of auditory processing disorder, it is not just an inability to filter sounds that are spoken to a person with the disability, but all types of language processing are disrupted. So when a person is attempting to take notes, they have to listen to the teachers' words and then write down what the teacher is saying; often while she is still talking. Because the learner hears the words he or she is writing, everything the teacher is saying while the notes are being written is not heard. Then once the notes are written down, the learner will try to reconnect with what the teacher is saying.

As a trainer, coming in to work with learners who are attempting to do this on a daily basis, what I see is a great deal of fatigue on their part. Even the ones who have not given up on learning are exhausted by this process. Often, it is written into IEP's and 504's that the learners should be given the notes, but teachers are reluctant to do this. They fear that giving them the notes will result in less attention being paid to lecture. I also find that after several attempts, the students no longer ask for the written notes and just do their best to follow along; often falling further and further behind.

Figure 5.1

Decoding Deficit
They do not seem to hear. What?

- Difficulty with new concepts or vocabulary
- Do better when visual clues are present
- Report trouble in group learning settings
- Academic problems often exist in tasks involving reading, decoding, spelling, note taking and following directions.

A child who can spell a word like it sounds probably has good decoding skills.

The next presentation of auditory processing disorder is called integration. (fig. 5.2) These students have trouble with multi-sensory input, often finding it overwhelming. They are more sensitive to new situations and have a tendency to take things at a slower pace. When other kids are eager to take on new challenges, these learners tend to be a little more cautious. Think about Teddy on the wall at PE and playing musical chairs.

While some teachers appreciate the break in schedule that an assembly can cause, others know that the rest of the day following the assembly will be impossible for some of the learners. The students who thrive in and crave routine are often off all day when the schedule changes and can even be visibly upset by the changes.

One of my students seems to take this to the extreme. Her mom picked her up from training one day and said that changing her routine caused her extreme distress. Mom reported that she had shown up to pick her daughter up earlier than expected from a friends' house. Her reaction had been, and often was, to throw a very childlike temper tantrum. Mom was desperate for help with her 14 year old daughter.

For kids who don't hear or see the world the same way most of us do, life seems to happen to them; they don't have much control. Other students hear the teacher say, '5 more minutes of work time' or 'it's time to finish up'. They hear and comprehend it when the teacher says, 'get out your books, turn to page 47 and look at the caption under the picture'. These students spend most of their day trying to play catch up and becoming frustrated, they never feel like they have control over the situation. When they are home, they feel more safe and relaxed and in control, until their schedules change. At times like that, they may over react because they feel they have lost control again.

Those who have trouble with integration are the ones who struggle to come up answers when called on. The ability to come up with 'on the spot' answers requires several senses to work together simultaneously. They have to hear and process the question, come up with an answer, verbalize the answer in their head, hold it in short term memory until the right time and then answer correctly. The inability to come up with answers at the spur of the moment like that can lead to stress, which further exacerbates the problem until it becomes stressful every time the teacher even begins to call on students.

Figure 5.2

Integration

Represents a deficit in tasks that require multisensory
input
"It's too much."

- They are the last ones to start a task, preferring to watch
  everyone else and follow their lead.
- They need more time for transitions.
- They don't seem to answer questions easily when called
  on.
- Academically, they struggle with reading, spelling and
  writing.

They seem to do better with tasks involving memorizing but
poor with tasks like sentence structure. Often have reversal
of digits.

To me, the most difficult presentation of auditory processing disorder to work with is called prosodic. (fig. 5.3) Those who have difficulty with the prosodic presentation are the ones who struggle the most since they also tend to have trouble socially. When I first realized that Seth had this presentation of APD, I was heartbroken. I realized that the perfect world I had set up for my little boy didn't exist to him. No matter how loved and accepted he was to those who we allowed him to be around, he did not have the ability to hear the tones of their voices the way they were being presented. Not only was he having trouble understanding the tones and innuendos of the language around him, I could not even ask him what he had heard or seen because the only way he knew was what he had been hearing all his life; which was people being harsh with him and yelling at him. It is his difficulties with this presentation that caused Seth to be the little boy who sat in the back corner of his second grade classroom and cried if someone spoke to him. It is the prosodic presentation that causes Seth to struggle to understand a lot of what goes on around him and spend many a night reviewing his perception of what happened in the hall or at baseball practice or in class and comparing that to what probably happened. While the misunderstandings can be amusing at times, they can also be difficult and painful for those who struggle with this presentation.

An amusing example was one day following a visit to a friend's house. He had been discussing the chores he is expected to complete at home. Since he is the oldest of four and we live on small acreage with chickens and a cow and a garden and a historic home, undergoing a complete renovation that we heat with wood, there are a lot of expectations for chores and tasks that need to be completed. Seth's friends' father mentioned that he needed to send his daughter over to our home on Saturday morning so she could see what it really was like to have to work. That Saturday morning, Seth awoke and began spurring us on to clean the house. He was convinced that the young lady was going to be sent over to the house to learn. We spent quite a bit of time trying to explain that the father was being sarcastic to no avail. He kept cleaning to get ready for the visitor. The appointed time came and went and Seth was disappointed that he did not have the expected help in completing his chores; which included splitting a large stack of wood.

At an in-service I led, I was approached by a teacher. She had identified one of her middle school students as at risk for having auditory processing disorder. The teacher also noted that the student was struggling socially; to the point that she often cried when approached by other students and always seemed to take things wrong. The teacher wanted to know if prosodic presentation could be this bad for a middle school student. My answer was a resounding yes! When a student has trouble understanding the tones and innuendos in all of their interactions with other students and with teachers, a school setting can be overwhelming, exhausting and emotional.

Associative (fig. 5.4) is probably one of the more frustrating for a classroom teacher to deal with and understand. This is the kid who gets one thing done and then turns to you with a blank expression. "Open your book to page 27 and do problems 1-23 odd. Work silently and I will come around and check how you are doing." The teacher finishes up at her desk and begins the rounds. The child is sitting at his desk with his book open to the wrong page and nothing on his paper. As his teacher, you assume he is not paying attention, is not motivated and is not following directions when in truth, he has opened his book to what he thought was right and didn't want to lean over and ask his neighbors a yet another question and is exhausted from trying so hard to keep up.

Figure 5.3

Prosodic

This problem may be more outwardly apparent than any of the others.

"He yelled at me."

- They don't have the ability to correctly use their voices to reflect rhythm, tone or volume.
- They are unable to recognize the variances in other people's voices.
- Because of this inability, they often have social problems.

Children may report not liking music and will often use an incorrect multisyllable word or leave parts of the words out. (aminal for animal or basketti for spaghetti)

One of my students suffers from this form more than others I have seen. I got to his house for a training session. We sat at the table and he proudly said, "Mrs. Holland, guess what? I have a new girlfriend." I responded, "You do, what is her name?" After what had to be a 20 second pause, he got out his phone and started scrolling through his contact list. When he got to her name on his list, he held up the phone and showed it to me. Now, with this student, I have learned to give him all the time he needs to come up with an answer, but this one really struck me. I had not initiated the conversation. I had not asked an out of line question, but he really could not come up with the answer.

To be in a classroom setting and be called on would be terrifying. If everything is working right, he can come up with answers to questions and can hold normal conversations. If it is not, he can't do it. The processing is just not there that allows his brain to pull random information out and articulate an answer; even when the information is in there. It is the associative presentation that is most often linked to the problems between reading and comprehension. When this same student reads, he is only slightly behind his peers on grade level. At 15, he reads on the 8th grade level. He can now quite successfully read out loud and can put an articulate thought on paper when he chooses the subject matter. But when the information is new or the vocabulary is not understandable, his comprehension is just not there. He often has absolutely no idea what he has read.

With these students, we often find that they do better early in school where the demands are not as high and struggle more as the demands on their auditory learning increase. In elementary school, they can rely more on the manipulatives and pictures to fill in what they missed from the classroom teaching. Since the

Figure 5.4

Associative

There is a slow down in the processing causing person to feel lost.
"Huh?"

- These kids start on the first step of a task you have given and then turn and look for help.
- Often need clarification when many directions have been given.
- Can often read, but have no idea what they have read- poor comprehension.
- Math word problems are difficult for them.
- Do fine in early school, but have more difficulty as the demands increase.

---

students intelligence level is often average to above average, they can catch on to the non verbal parts of the lessons and figure it out. As they get older, these cues are often no longer in our learning environments. We have to rely more and more on reading materials and listening to lectures making it more difficult for these students to stay on task, focus, concentrate and keep up. All of these circumstances increase their level of frustration.

The fifth type is termed the output-organization presentation. (fig. 5.5) When students struggle in this manner, they are having difficulty with tasks that involve executive function. Executive function is the ability to make a plan and follow through with that plan. If you tell the students to prepare for their labs, most will follow the set of instructions you have previously reviewed to complete that task and be successful at it. There are always those one or two students who are always completely unprepared. They have to be reminded over and over again what to do. The multi-step directions just don't seem to click. These are also the students who arrive every day without needed supplies. They are my student Rachel who carries everything on her back all the time so she won't forget. Or another of my students who has forgotten things so many times that he suffers from intense anxiety about going through the halls and to his locker; so much so that it is written on his IEP that he can leave class early to avoid the noise and confusion in the halls.

Because those with output-organization struggles often throw things together, they seem to be the kids whose desk is always stuffed full of everything whose lockers will not shut because everything is crammed in. Binders, provided to help organize are haphazardly thrown together with nothing anywhere that allows it to be found.

Picture your mind as being like a card catalog. We have pieces of information in there that are organized and can be pulled in an organized manner when certain information is required. In the student with out-put organization difficulties, the cards in their catalog have not been put in any order. They are all in there, but they were all just stuffed in. So, when a person who struggles in this manner and is given new information, it gets into the brain, but is not filed in an organized manner, it becomes harder to retrieve. When these students write notes, they often mirror what is happening in their brain and are hard to make sense of. When this student is asked to provide either written or oral responses, especially on the spot, they often fail.

Think about what it is like to try to remember a persons name you haven't seen in a couple of years or recall the hotel you once stayed at. You stand there thinking, 'what is her name?' Your blank mind struggles to come up with information you know you have. Often, several hours later when you are completing an unrelated task, the name will pop into your head. For a student with output organization difficulties, this is what their life is like all day, every day.

Figure 5.5

Output-Organization
The executive function struggles in kids with this presentation.

"I don't know!"

- Have trouble with sequenced information such as directions or step by step tasks
- The information goes in, but is not organized in a way that allows the child to process it correctly or give an appropriate response.
- These children also have trouble organizing their personal space as well as lockers, schedules and desks.
- Notes are often non-existent or lack organization enough to be made sense of.
- Students have trouble organizing thoughts and often stumble on words and phrases when trying to express themselves.

Chapter 6

How is the Learner Affected?

On one of the occasions when my kids switched schools, I had a conversation with school personnel regarding why we were switching schools. I replied that my boys had APD and they would receive more services at a public school than they would at the private school they had been attending. His response was, "APD? Isn't that what men get on Sunday afternoons when the football game is on?" His attempt at humor, while infuriating, was also an eye opener on how very little the condition is understood.

I am going to try to provide you with some sense of what 'hearing' with auditory processing disorder sounds like. Imagine buying a ticket and going to the movies. It is a pretty good investment of time and money and expectations are probably pretty high. The movie starts with some fantastic graphics, but no sound. You figure it is probably just some publicity stunt and stay seated. The opening credits begin and so does the movie, but you only hear every third or fourth word. The actors' lips are moving all the time but all you hear is the rustling of candy wrappers, ice in drink cups and people shifting in their seats. How long until your patience is gone?

Now imagine you are five or six or seven years old and the event is a 7 hour long school day. The teachers' words come in fine sometimes, but at other times you can only hear the fan for the smart board. You have trouble concentrating because kids keep getting up to get things they need or ask the teacher questions. Before you know it, the other kids are ahead of you in school and getting better grades. You are bored and fidgety. You lose patience. You try to participate but only hear part of the question and answer wrong and the kids laugh. Auditory processing disorder is a big deal for a kid and a lot more than the Sunday afternoon football game scenario.

Auditory processing difficulties show up twice as often in men as in women, but it is not something that can just be written off as just a guy thing. It is estimated that as many as 7% of all children have difficulties with their auditory processing and as high as 9% of the total population struggles with some form of processing difficulties, whether that be auditory, sensory integration, visual, concept or tactile. To me, that makes it a difference, rather than a disorder. As parents and as educators we need to figure out how to best educate this 9% of the population. We can't teach and not have them hear and blame them for bad behavior. We can't ignore this learning difference and blame them for low performance and test scores. We can't change the way they learn any more than we can change the way that we do, but we can change the way that we present information to

54

allow for more of our students become successful in the class-room and in life.

As my research continues to develop, I realize that there is a wide array of areas affected by learning disabilities and that they are all encompassing. In other words, it is not just dyslexics that struggle with written expression, but all learning disabilities tend to present with a tendency to struggle with written expression. It is not just those with auditory processing disorders who struggle with short term memory, but all those with learning disabilities tend to struggle with short term memory. Executive function difficulties do not just affect those with dysgraphia, but all learning disabled seem to struggle with it. While it is not a given that having a learning disability means that the person will struggle with these areas, each of these needs to be considered when we are trying to figure out how best to serve each individual.

What are these common areas and how are they affected? While not a complete list, the most common areas affected are: short term memory, language skills, math (especially word problems and problem solving), anxiety, comprehension, executive function, processing, organization and social cues. Following is a brief explanation of how the learner is affected in these areas.

Short term memory is commonly affected. Short term memory is generally described as the information we hold on to for 5 minutes or less. Our second son Benjamin struggles with this one. It is why we called him squirrel for years. We would give him a task, such as "Go out to the barn, get into the white cabinet and get the hammer." Ben would go out into the barn and we would have to send someone out after Ben because he had been distracted by a thought and had forgotten the task at hand. In the classroom, those who have difficulties with short term memory often get the first step of a set of directions and then are at a loss. They get out their math book and stop and look for direction. These are also often the kids who need to have assignments broken down in small pieces for them. They never seem to have what they need for class. They get to their lockers, put things away and remember to grab about half of what they need. Remember Rachel and her back pack that weighs almost as much as she does. For another of my students, the locker causes him more than lost points. The thought of going to his locker and not being able to open it or forgetting something causes him such anxiety that he is not able to pass between classes with his peers.

Often when we think about auditory processing disorders, we think about a person who has trouble hearing at parties or when background noise is present. But as we have already discussed, spoken language, written language and composed language are all 'heard' as they are used and background noise interrupts all of them; not just the spoken/heard language. So when language problems exist, they can be in all areas of language. What can be confusing to those working with kids who have learning disabilities is that sometimes, there don't seem to be problems and sometimes, they are overwhelming to the learner. Compounding this struggle is that there does not seem to be any way to determine when they will be ok and when they will struggle.

The learning disability dyscalculia refers to difficulties in comprehending and understanding math skills. Similar to dyslexia, dyscalculia affects the perception of numbers and spatial relationships so that following the sequence of numbers becomes a task in futility. If sequencing is a problem, so are things like time, money and mathematical equations. Try to imagine scheduling your day, either in your mind or on paper, if the concept of time does not make sense. Trying to figure out things like how early you need to wake up in the morning if you need to leave 30 minutes early is difficult if the numbers don't make sense. Making and keeping appointments, figuring out how to set goals for projects and breaking complex tasks into smaller manageable pieces are all tasks that involve the use of sequencing and require a basic understanding and comprehension of time. For a student, managing time in the classroom becomes a huge problem. Most students are able to look at the clock and keep track of how much time is left to take a test or complete a task on time and plan accordingly. They can also look at the clock and come to a good stopping point in an assignment or reading would be. For the student who struggles with these concepts, the classroom can be a frustrating place.

Never having books closed or supplies put away when the bell rings or being at a good stopping point puts the student behind and flustered when leaving the classroom; behind when getting to the locker and often late getting to or arriving when the bell rings and beginning unprepared for the next class. Imagine not understanding numbers and trying to open a locker or having a separate combination for the locker in the gym. Even a task as simple as 'go to the third door on the left and ask the janitor for the mop bucket' becomes a task wrought with stress. Tasks that are simple and commonplace for the average learner become lessons in humiliation and stress for a student who struggles with math concepts.

I went to the grocery store one day. In front of me was an older man who was paying for several items he had purchased.

56

The lady at the register told him, 'that will be $5.36.' The man opened his wallet and took out several bills. He handed the lady a $10 bill and looked at her for approval. The lady nodded her head. He opened up his change container and dumped his change out into his hand and held it out to her and she counted out loud, but took only what she needed for him to pay his bill.

This type of encounter is a reality for a person with dyscalculia. Imagine being an adult and being unable to manage a bank account. When writing a check, making a deposit or tracking a debit, it would be hard to figure out if you needed to add or subtract. Not knowing if you wrote the numbers down correctly or struggling to figure out where to put the period could drastically change the outcome and the stress involved in paying your bills. The prospect of going to Walmart or any other big chain grocery store would be daunting and overwhelming. To many mistakes could result in your bank account being closed and having to rely on the kindness of strangers to take only the bills and change from your outstretched hand that were needed to pay your bill and then to give you back your change.

Sometimes, it is not just the difficulties of the learning disability that cause the difficulties of the learners. I spend a lot of time talking with the learners about their experiences to try to begin fully understand what is happening in their minds so I can best help them. For example, one student I was working with was having a great deal of difficulty at school and his parents did not know why. He had been diagnosed with APD, which is why he was seeing me, but that did not fully explain his sudden anxieties and lack of concern for school work that was being observed at home and at school.

When questioned, it was discovered that the situation at home was so overwhelming that even being at school was stressful for him because he was preoccupied by thoughts of what was happening at home in his absence. For another of my students, the word math causes such ingrained responses that his stress reaction is instantaneous. A stress, such as these, causes the hormone cortisol to be released. For the one student, as soon as I pulled out a math sheet, he began tapping his foot and fidgeting. Cortisol functions in two different ways for memory. The first is that when cortisol is present, the brain has difficulty retrieving information from long term memory. A learner who is experiencing anxiety will most likely have a more difficult time coming up with answers for information they know. Think of times when you are anxious and your mind seems to draw a blank. For some, this happens when faced with something like speaking in public. For others, it may be going to a

57

party. Still others will stress over getting on the school bus or going into a classroom. The excess cortisol released in response to anxiety temporarily changes the way your mind treats memories. The same cortisol that makes it hard to retrieve information also makes it impossible for information to enter into long term memory. So when my student hears the word math, his anxiety level goes into overdrive and cortisol is released. This cortisol does a couple of things for his learning. One is that it makes it extremely hard for him to come up with answers when he is asked to answer a question either in class or in the session. For those who have had this happen a few times, the anxiety level goes up even at the thought of the class when there is a high likelihood that the student will be put into that situation. Secondly, since his anxiety level is already up, it will be impossible to retain any information from one class to the next because the cortisol will serve as a block. For a lot of learning disabled students, who are forced into uncomfortable situations in a typical classroom environment, this is what is happening to them all day every day.

Another factor that sets in and affects the student in different ways is the level of exhaustion they are experiencing on any given day. . For a student with a learning disorder who has had to take notes or has struggled to understand a new concept, the process can be overwhelming and exhausting. For a student with auditory processing disorder, even in a class where there were several sets of directions given orally to complete a task; such as science labs, listening over noise to ensure success is difficult. For a student with dyslexia, the process of taking notes or doing a task which requires visual attention causes the same stress. Just imagine that you are daily faced with being forced into circumstances that cause you stress and think about how you would feel at the end of the day. That exhaustion is very apparent in Ben. Some days he comes home fine. Some days he needs some time and space to decompress before he faces the rest of the world. I see this with my clients too.

Often, these students are seen as 'not performing up to their potential' or 'just needing to buckle down and apply themselves.' When in truth, the actual task of just listening, looking or attending to the task at hand is exhausting, causes stress hormones to be released and becomes quickly overwhelming. I have been asked why these students don't tell people they can't hear what is going on or can't see the letters like they should. Have you ever heard it said that you can't ask a blind man what the color blue looks like? This is a similar problem. If the student has always heard everything going on around them; how does he

58

know the way he hears is not normal? If she has always had the letters swim all around the page when she is looking at it, how does she know that yours line up in perfect rows? If school has always been tedious and exhausting for her, how does she know that it is easy for most of the kids she is in class with? Being learning disabled is having nothing wrong with his intelligence level, but having a brain that takes information in a way that does not line up with the way the teacher is trying to teach and being more and more frustrated and confused by what he knows he should be able to understand. It has nothing to do with not applying herself or being lazy or her ability and everything to do with the way she is being taught.

One of the more confusing symptoms of learning disabilities is that of not being able to comprehend what has been read or heard. I have one student with APD who reads close to grade level but comprehends almost none of what he reads. He reads with proper tones and inflections and his voice is not choppy or broken when he reads. If asked the most basic level compre-hension questions after the passage, such as what is the passage about, he cannot tell you if he read about penguins or the State of Missouri. His comprehension is almost nonexistent. Having the material read to him in a completely quiet setting helps his comprehension a great deal. Remember that if he is reading, he can hear the voice in his head. If it is completely quiet, he can hear only that voice, there is no competition and it is easier for him to comprehend. If there is background noise present, he hears all the other sounds and his comprehension slips. The more other sounds present, the less comprehension he has. For other learning disabilities, the inability to comprehend can be linked to difficulty with short term memory or working memory. Remember that to comprehend a sentence; the learner must be able to make sense of each word until he gets to the end of the sentence and each sentence until he gets to the end of a para-graph and each paragraph until he gets to the end of the chap-ter. If the class reads a section of a chapter out loud and a stu-dent struggles with this task, this type teaching style is not going to be the best for that student.

Earlier in the book, I introduced you to my husband and, in my description, described someone who is smart and hardwork-ing and helps other people make plans on a daily basis. But when it comes to making his own plans, he struggles. When working on our house, he literally requires at least one person on the ground running to get the things he has forgotten to get to complete the task at hand. Executive function is the part of our brain that allows us to make a plan and follow through with that plan. It allows us to figure out what we will need to carry out the task at hand or to break the plan down into small pieces and make it more manageable. Those who struggle with this task are the ones who never remember their pencil or their notebook or their calculator. They show up to class, often with just whatever supplies they carry around with them. For my husband, this results in him getting up on top of the scaffolding with only a tape measure and pencil and sending someone else running for the screwdriver, screws, wire and picture. For those who struggle with this skill even simple daily tasks can seem overwhelming. Figuring out what is needed from one class to the next is a struggle, but not nearly as much of a struggle as is the end of the day when the student is trying to figure out how to get ready to go home; what subjects he has homework in and which ones he can leave at school. Then once he has that figured out, he needs to figure out which books are needed for that homework, which notebooks, what the assignment is and whether or not other supplies are needed to complete those assignments. This process must be completed for each subject the student is involved all while trying to not miss the bus.

When executive function suffers, so does the ability to sort out and make sense of complex mathematical equations. Often the student who does fine in elementary school memorizing math problems struggles later in school when the memorizing gives way to breaking down and solving mathematical equations. The same student who does well when science experiments are written down and broken down for them in elementary school struggles when they have to conduct experiments and come up with variables on their own.

Chapter 7

A New Approach to IEPs/504s for Learning Disabled Students

"If a child can't learn the way we teach, maybe we should teach the way they learn."

-Ignacio Estrada

My eldest son, Seth, went to see the Superman movie "Man of Steel". The next morning, he told me, "Mom, guess what? Superman has APD." I asked him what gave him that idea? He replied, "He hears everything that goes on around him all the time and he has to really concentrate to hear what just one person is saying." First of all, I must admit, I bet the creators of the film did not realize they were giving their hero a 'disability'. Second of all, if it is a superhuman power in the movie, why is it a disability in the classroom? How can we find ways to utilize this superhuman power for the good and benefit of the learners?

Before you had a person in your life with a learning disability, how much did you know and understand about that learning disability? When you first heard the diagnosis, did you instantly know exactly what systems were going to be affected and how?

Yet, when we approach the IEP/504 meetings, we are often incensed that the teacher is not following the exact intent of every part of the IEP for our learner and his/her disability. We assume that the teaching certificate came with knowledge about every single way each and every student can be affected by each and every condition out there. We expect them to know how their classroom set up and approach will work with our learner and automatically know exactly how to care for and adapt the curriculum for our student and each of the other students in her care who also learns in a non-traditional way. Right? After all, the fact that the school and the district are required by law to test for and come up with these individualized education plans means that their time for each and every student in their care is limitless. Our child deserves an 'individualized education', more so even than the other 20 kids in the classroom do.

And the law states that all interested parties are to get together and go over the laundry list of all the different ways each student who has an IEP: has been tested under ideal circumstances, does or does not meet our minimum expectations or has or has not since he/she was born. I served as an advocate at one of these meetings where I listened to 45 minutes of every diagnosis and test that my client had been subjected to in kindergarten through 8th grade. I was angry when I left the meeting at the lack of respect shown for my time, the parents' time, the teacher's time and mostly the integrity and intelligence of my client, who was sitting next to me for the entire 45 minute meeting. The parents already knew all the information and the teachers could have been emailed a packet. Then we could have met and said, you all have read where he has been and what we have found in an educational setting that has been going on. What now? How can we best serve this young man, realistically, in the classroom? We have two experts here who work one on one with this student and they are going to briefly go over some of the ways his learning style affects him in the classroom. Then we will all put our heads together and come up with a plan to in-sure we help him succeed.

Unfortunately, I believe IEP's look at the areas of weakness and then cater to them. As mentioned earlier, these are often average to above average IQ students who are struggling be-cause of the way their minds take in information. They don't need to have only half the curriculum presented to them or to be pulled out for 50% of their day. They need to find ways to suc-ceed.

Albert Einstein said, "I never teach my pupils, I only provide the conditions in which they can learn." When we assume we have the knowledge each student needs and can, through books and quizzes make that knowledge stick in them, we are doing a disservice to what our job is as educators. If it is our job to dump the information in so that they can perform well on a cer-tain test, we are fine. If it is our job to inspire the mind to open up and make connections and flourish, we are often failing. We may be getting those scores where we need them, but the stu-dents need to have opportunities to figure stuff out on their own and then grow and learn from their experiences. How are our classrooms providing the opportunities our students' need in which they can learn?

One of the quotes I recently saw came from a learning disa-bled student. It was, "My brain is like the Bermuda Triangle. In-formation goes in and is never found again." In the minds of those who take information in differently, or the learning disa-bled, the connections are often not made between the old infor-mation and the new. Unfortunately, it is that information; those connections that make the random facts make sense. If the pieces of information in the brain are not connected and orga-nized, the brain struggles to come up with the pieces it needs when it needs them. The processing is affected.

As I sit and work with my students, that is what I am trying to figure out. For one of my students, it is that she learned her numbers and knows some addition and multiplication. Where is the rest of it and how do I get it to stick? How can I make those connections? I have the privilege of working with my students' one on one and can spend time and energy and effort concentrating on each learner to figure this out. My job is to provide an individualized education to each of my students while helping them learn to compensate for the unique way in which their mind works. The classroom teacher's job is quite different. She has been given a specific set of information that her students must learn in a given time. Her job is to figure out how to best present that information so that the highest number of students possible will comprehend what they need to know and do her best to make all the accommodations recommended by the 504 and IEP kids in her classroom. She often does this without the benefit of understanding exactly what ways those learning disabilities affect the overall learner, but rather the set of guidelines she has been given about the ways the learner is going to struggle with what she is teaching.

When we have learners in our classroom who struggle to learn in a traditional way, they often do not see a reason for what they are trying to learn and give up. The more they are struggling in a given subject, the more likely they are to stop trying to succeed. The student who struggles to recall basic addition and subtraction facts is not going to try to master algebra. A student who has trouble memorizing facts is not going to diligently memorize and recall the Bill of Rights or the Preamble of the Constitution or the states and capitals. Part of our job as educators is to realize what the learners' goals are and then find ways to help them see how what we are teaching them gets them to their goals.

This year, one of my students did not see how or why she should understand government. Her goal in life is to marry a rich doctor, live in a huge house with her salon attached and be a hair dresser to the stars. Why would she ever need to understand government? We began to look at taxes and laws made that could concern her. We talked about how, if she was totally ignorant of how the system worked, she could end up loosing not only her studio, but her husband could loose his income as a doctor. We looked at political candidates and tried to figure out how we could begin to make choices depending on how the candidates' beliefs could affect our lives as cosmetologist and doctor. She also didn't see why it was so important for her to learn her math. She could figure stuff out with a calculator couldn't she? We began to discuss a scenario in which a customer wanted to get color and highlights, but insisted on using a specific formula in her hair. What did she need to know to make sure she was charging enough? Of course with a teenage girl, I also point out that she needs to be able to figure out how much items cost when they are on sale so she learns how many new sparkly tank tops she can afford. As I mentioned earlier, I have the privilege of working with these students one on one, so I can individualize their learning in this manner. A classroom teacher does not have that same ability for each lesson with each of the 20 learners every hour for the 6 classes she teaches.

What needs to happen? I go back to that meeting I sat through where we listened to a laundry list of what my client cannot do and see a different scenario. In the new scenario, the student, the current teachers and last years teachers, the parents, administrators and any interested parties sit down together before the beginning of the school year and go over expectations for what the student needs to accomplish to successfully pass the class. All parties involved discuss what parts might pose challenges for the learner and find solutions that might help the student succeed.

After that, the same team needs to meet quarterly to go over what parts the student is succeeding with and where the student still needs help or is struggling. The team sets new goals based on the successes and struggles of the individual learner. Parents and students agree to do their part to help the teacher succeed and not be overwhelmed. Meetings can be called by either the parents or the teacher if the student seems to be having particular struggles in between the quarterly scheduled times. At the end of the school year, progress and successes are reviewed and noted while areas of concern are highlighted. Plans for summer work are made and agreed upon by the student and parents to continue forward progress.

When the IEP's/504's are made to focus on the success of the learner rather than on their failures and all are involved and agree upon the expected outcomes, the learner will begin to take responsibility for his or her own learning while focusing on forward progress. When the learner begins to take on this responsibility and understand that all are working towards the common goal of his or her success, learning is more likely to occur.

Chapter 8

Neuroplasticity, Brain Training and All That Good Stuff

Let's begin with a science lesson, not a very detailed one, but good enough to give us an idea of how this stuff works. If you want more details, find my page "Treating APD" on Facebook and I will occasionally post articles and more detailed information about why this works there.

We are born with about a billion little dendrites and neurons in our brains. Let's think about the neurons like branches and dendrites like the leaves. As we grow and learn, those dendrites and neurons begin to come together into groups that make sense and help us function. When you are first born, your neurons fire all over the place. For a mental image, think about a newborn baby with arms and legs moving all over and very little control over movement. As the brain continues to develop, the dendrites that control our large muscles begin to form paths that make sense and the baby begins to be able to control his/her muscle movements. The more often those paths are followed, the better that connection is made, so that eventually we gain control over our bodies.

The neurons and dendrites that are used the most often form into a firm foundation, like a solid tree truck with branches and leaves going out into our bodies. The neurons and dendrites we use all the time are made more solid by making strong connections, the ones we do not use fall away and eventually die. Think of it as pruning the trees of unwanted limbs that stick out funny or have died.

We develop the neuron and dendrite patterns in our bodies in predictable patterns for the most part. But sometimes, either through genetic makeup or illness or life events, the path is not forged the way it should. For example, if a child is around the age of 18 months, the body is hard wired to concentrate on the development of language skills. If, during that time, the child has three ear infections that result in fluid being in the ears for an extended period of time, the child may fall a bit behind in language acquisition. If the family has a car accident and someone is hurt and the child spends an extraordinary amount of time in front of the television at that time instead of communicating, those skills may fall behind. If the child is genetically predisposed to have those neurons from the ear to the brain run a little differently, those patterns may not be heard quite right and the language skills may suffer.

Studies on neuroplasticity originated when we began treating people who had suffered strokes or traumatic brain injuries. We learned that when a particular area of the brain was damaged, and a skill set was lost, work could often be done to find new paths to regain the lost skills. Scanning the brain activity showed us that the new path was different than the old one had been, but the task was still being successfully completed. A person who had lost the ability to read could be taught to read again. If we scanned the brain of a person who had not had a stroke, we would find certain areas of the brain firing away in a predictable pattern when he/she was reading. A book placed in front of a person who had been injured in that part of the brain showed that those connections were no longer working. The person might know they should be able to read, but the brain was not firing to make them have that ability. If the person was determined to read, over time, the brain would start to fire again.

Often, it was different areas of the brain that were firing and the damaged part was being bypassed. The brain was making new connections and learning to read all over again. When the person was a successful reader, it was found that the way the brain fired up again when reading material was placed in front of them was quite different from that of a normal brain person, but the result was successful reading none the less.

The research was fascinating. Where old knowledge told us that an old dog can't learn new tricks, new research told us that it could and it could be successful in that learning. The question then became what are the limits of the brain?

As we look then at the learning patterns that exist within society, we find a wide variety of what is acceptable and considered normal. Talk to a group of people about learning and you will hear some say something like, "I am such a visual learner" while another points out, "I am totally hands on" and another says something like, "I just need to be able to read it two or three times." These people are expressing that they prefer to learn things or learn them best visually, through tactile means or through auditory channels. Each brain is wired to learn a little differently and yet most teachers teach others the way that they learn best. For learners with different styles, they may find those classes with those who teach differently difficult to understand. When you throw in those who have distinct learning disabilities, it becomes even more challenging.

The easiest way to think about brain training/neuroplasticity is that the brain works like any group of muscles in our bodies. For example, if we want to get a 6 pack wash board looking stomach, we must work those ab muscles 5 times a week for several months while eating the right way and getting our weight ideal. For the brain to make new connections, they must be forged and then maintained to work properly. Go back to the ab scenario. If we work the abs for a period of time and get the results we want, we have forged new connections and increased the working ability of those muscles. They are now capable of doing things they couldn't do before.

If we are working with a person who has poor short term memory, we can work that short term memory over and over again until the brain realizes that it is going to be required to use it. The brain will forge new paths to make the work easier and eventually it will be able to use that new path on a regular basis and the short term memory will become a tool the person will be able to count on and use on a regular basis. Let's move back to the stomach scenario. If we get the 6 pack, look in the mirror and take a picture and then sit on the couch for the next two months eating chips and ice cream, what happens to that 6 pack? It is the same for the brain. If we work on and develop a new connection and force the brain to take new pathways to acquiring or strengthening a skill set, attain those goals and then quit using it, we will loose it again.

This can happen to those who plug their kids into a computer program to obtain results. They complete the program, but don't explain to their learner why they have to do it, just that they have to; they have no buy in to what is happening or why. They take a test that says the results have been attained and then they stop working the brain. Six months later, they find that the brain has 'forgotten' the new skill. What has happened, in actuality is that a new path was formed when the brain was being asked repeatedly to complete a task. A new branch was formed with dendrites snaking out to the correct places to complete the task. When the path was not used, the branch weakened and the dendrites fell away. The task is relearned and the results are permanent when the purpose for the learning is explained to the student, the student buys into and understands what is happening and then measures are taken to make sure the learning is maintained. If the 'training' happens and is successful before the age of 9, the changes in the way the brain handles new information can be permanent.

Chapter 9

Treatment

The good news is that treatment is possible for those with learning disabilities. We can change the way the brain works and responds to stimulus. In chapter 8, we looked, very briefly, at neuroplasticity and brain training. If a person has auditory processing disorder, we can provide them with a regular workout program for the ears and brain that encourages the brain to forge a new path for that information to travel. If we work that path out on a regular basis and explain why we are doing what we are doing and have the buy in we need, we can train the brain to respond to auditory stimulus in a new way and 'hear' things they couldn't hear before. If a person is dyslexic, we can provide the eyes with a regular training program that works the area of the brain responsible for organizing visual clues until they start to have the written word begin to make sense. Once it does, we can continue the exercises to make sure the new path stays strong.

What we also know about those with learning disabilities is that they tend to struggle with other skills necessary for learning such as comprehension, short term memory, executive function, note taking and recall. To correctly treat each learner, we must first identify the areas the learner struggles with then find ways to incorporate games and activities to work all the areas of the brain in as short of a time as possible to have a maximum impact on the learner.

Through observation and testing, you should be able to determine in what areas your student struggles. If, for example, your APD student struggles with visual cues, short term memory and comprehension, you should cater your training session to address all of those areas at every session. As with any workout routine, the more often the plan is followed, the more likely it is to be successful. It is also necessary for the learner to know why they are doing what they are doing. Let's go back, for a second to the stomach muscles analogy. If you decide your husband needs a 6 pack washboard stomach and every night, after he goes to sleep, you hook up a machine that stimulates the muscles needed for the 6 pack for an hour. He has no interest in getting the 6 pack; no buy in to what is happening and continues to drink his 32 ounce big gulp and eat donuts and fries every day while at work. You might see results for the short term, but if he is not doing the work, he will return to the same gut in front of the television you have been seeing for years.

Really, it is the same for brain training. If we tell a person we are going to play games every day for 45 minutes and they can get ice cream when they are done, they may cooperate and play the games for the short term and there may even be a difference in the ability of that person, but once they get tired of the games, everything will go back to the way it was. We must tell the person we are working with what the purpose of each activity is. They must understand and buy in to what is happening.

I refer to the work sessions we are doing as training sessions, since we are working out the brain and bulking up on those skills we are 90 pound weaklings on. For a person who has APD, terrible short term memory and trouble with comprehension, a training session would consist of the following parts:

1. warm up/stress relief
2. comprehension
3. short term memory
4. auditory training
5. comprehension revisited
6. activity

If the person has APD and dyslexia as well as executive function issues and short term memory difficulties, a training session might look like this:

1. warm up/stress relief
2. visual exercises
3. executive function training
4. auditory training
5. short term memory work
6. activity

Notice that the session needs to be changed to meet the needs of each person. In the next several chapters, we will outline activities that can be used for type of struggle the typical learning disabled person has. While the list is extensive, it is not comprehensive and I add new activities to my repertoire every time I research. To stay informed on the latest developments, find 'Treating APD' on Facebook. I will add links to research and other relevant information as well as pose questions to illicit conversation about learning disabilities.

When we look at the most effective methods of getting information to any learner, we need to provide a multisensory approach. While that buzzword has been going around for many years, the necessity of the approach may not have been thoroughly explained.

The most effective methods of learning for everyone involve a multisensory approach. If you hear a new piece of information verbally one time, let's say a phone number, how likely are you

73

to remember that phone number? If you hear the phone number and write it down, you are more likely to remember it even if you loose the piece of paper. If you hear the phone number and write it down and look at it several times you will probably remember it. The first approach involved only one sense, auditory. Hearing and writing it down involved two senses, auditory and tactile. The third approach involved three senses, auditory, visual and tactile. When the information goes into the brain in three different ways, rather than one, the brain has more sources to pull it from and is more likely to remember it.

In the classroom, it is actually why students may falter with upper level math, but are able to be successful with upper level science. A good science teacher will present the information in lecture form, providing opportunities for the students to take notes and provide a visual stimulus with a presentation and then follow up with an experiment to demonstrate. The student's senses will all be stimulated and they are much more likely to remember because of it. On the other hand, upper level math courses are based mostly on lecture, note taking and memorization of formulas and do not involve a multisensory approach, making upper level math harder for learners to grasp.

With all we have learned about students who suffer with processing disorders, let's go back to the first approach of taking in information. You hear a phone number one time and you have an auditory processing disorder with a speech in noise level of hearing loss of 47%. You will only hear half of those numbers. If you have a tendency towards dyslexia with that auditory processing issue, you will only hear half of what is said and may transpose two of the numbers. As teachers and parents, we need to figure out which approaches work best for each student and then make those approaches the norm in the classroom.

The following is a chart that shows two different approaches to presenting vocabulary. Even with vocabulary, notice how many of these strategies engage the brain and use a multisensory approach to teaching the new information.

10 Tips for Effectively Teaching Vocabulary

Do This:	Not This:
1. Select words to teach.	1. Assign a list of words weekly from a set book.
2. Spend time every day engaging students in word studies that help the words make sense and give them an interest in the words chosen.	2. Have students write words a set number of times, look them up in the dictionary or make up sentences using the words.
3. Help the students come up with definitions that make sense to them while explaining the words.	3. Have students copy definitions from the board or a dictionary.
4. Assess the students understanding of the new vocabulary by encouraging them to use the terms correctly in their everyday writing.	4. Test students' ability to memorize information by having them match words to definitions.
5. Teach the students about the words, the meanings of the parts of the words and the ways we can learn about words in relation to each other.	5. Encourage students to use the context to figure out what the words are and what they mean.
6. Use pictures, hand gestures and graphics to help students make up their own vocabulary reminders.	6. Use the words in isolation and have them learn them on their own to make sure they have the words memorized.
7. Use a word wall in the classroom that utilizes structures to help the students' link the words to other words. Use pictures and other graphics as visual aids and reminders.	7. Do not have or misuse the word wall in the classroom.
8. As a teacher, use the words in everyday learning. Have the students listen for the words being used in everyday lessons.	8. Focus on tools that highlight the words in isolation.
9. Look for readings that contain the words to help link the words in real world context.	9. Have the kids write the words over and over again to try to help memorize.
10. The teacher constantly models the use of good grammar skills and encourages the students to do the same.	10. Talk to the kids using only their language and slang and accept the same from them.

Some time ago, I was privileged to be able to spend a day observing a student in his classroom as he went through his day to day routine at school. His classroom teacher and I talked about her observations and concerns for this student before school started. During that time, the teacher 'warned me' that the class would be taking a language arts test that day. Before the test, the material would be reviewed. She explained to me that she would be utilizing a teaching strategy called whole brain teaching. She explained that she would be acting out a lot of material and the students would be very actively involved in the process.

At that point, I had not heard of whole brain teaching, but couldn't wait to find out. When we got to language arts, the teacher told the class to get ready to review for the test. Then she got their attention and they all responded exactly the same way. Then she began reviewing terms. She would say the term and make a motion. The kids repeated the motion and the words-exactly. When she got to the end of a section, the kids were told to teach. They immediately turned their chairs, paired up with another student and taught each other the material using the same words and the same motions. Not only were they getting an auditory, a visual and a kinesthetic cue, they were being taught to synthesize the information so that they could present it. They reviewed all the information for the test in this manner.

She then told them it was time to take the test. I walked around observing the students while they were testing. I watched them sit at their desks and make the hand motions to themselves and then fill in an answer. This was repeated by those kids who were struggling to finish their tests and the ones who were flying through.

If you are an educator and are not yet familiar with whole brain teaching, I highly recommend that you get on the internet and do a search. Whole brain teaching is an excellent tool for working with several types of learners in your classroom. It is a multi-sensory approach to education. The students hear the information spoken by the teacher. They watch her make a motion that in some way helps them connect to the information. They move their own bodies in that way; mimicking her moves. Then, they have to synthesize the information well enough to explain it to another student.

Needless to say, I LOVE whole brain teaching. This multi sensory approach allows one teacher to teach to the learning styles of more of the learning styles in the classroom. It will encourage you to go way beyond your comfort zone as a teacher and will engage more of your learners. Because it uses a multi-sensory approach, it also engages students who learn differently than you teach.

Think back to the information regarding neuroplasticity and brain training in the previous chapter, think again about that tree with the branches and leaves going out through the body. Now imagine that the ears, eyes, skin, vestibular, nose; that each has its own leaves going out. If a new piece of information moves a leaf coming from the eyes, the ears, the fingers and the vestibular system, how much more likely is it going to be to make an impression that will last in the body?

As we get into the next several chapters, we will look at ways to work with the main areas affecting the learner in the classroom and in life. Where I can, these methods utilize a multisensory approach to learning and teaching.

Chapter 10

Detox/Music Therapy

It was when I started scheduled visits with learners that I began to realize that some days we might as well not even meet; my students got so little out of the session. At first I was confused as to what could be causing some sessions to be almost perfect and others to be a disaster. I began to talk more to the learners about what was going on in their lives, especially when the session seemed to be such a struggle. What I discovered was that asking them the simple, "How was your day at school?" could elicit a wide range of information. I began to hear about teachers who did not understand and friends that made fun of them. I heard about stresses at home and stresses caused by regular life events. It caused me to begin to look into the effects of stress on the mind of the learner.

What I discovered is that the way the brain reacts to stress can prevent learning. Stress does not only hinder learning, but prevents it. Technically, when the frontal part of the brain, called the amygdala is in a state of stress or fear and is feeling anxiety, new information coming through the sensory intake areas of the brain CANNOT pass through the frontal area to gain access to the memory circuits. While this information is important to all learners, it is crucial to the success of students with learning disabilities. Since we know that regardless of quality, instruction is limited by the student's ability to retain and recall the information being taught, it becomes imperative that the learning environment be stress free allowing for each learner to achieve to his or her full potential. With all that we have learned about the affects of learning differences on the entirety of the brain including memory and comprehension, we might be able to begin to understand that importance of finding ways to decrease the stress the learner is feeling before we begin to teach.

For the sake of our training sessions, to be the most effective, the stress level also needs to be decreased allowing this flow of information to happen in the brain. By the time the students came to me, they had been dealing with normal stresses of every day life that were compounded by the stress of trying to fit into a regular classroom environment. Along with being stressful, coping with a regular learning environment is exhausting to students who may not have developed appropriate strategies for dealing with that stress, resulting in an ever compounding learning catastrophe. As we work with learning disabled students, we must learn to recognize the signs of stress and begin to teach and enforce the effective use of stress reducing strategies for them.

Empowering these students by teaching them to self-monitor and to advocate for themselves will make their learning experiences more meaningful and should result in better grades and better overall retention of material.

It was with this in mind that I began to research ways to decrease the stress level of the learner before we even began to meet our session objectives. What I found was music. Not just any music, but classical music with a calm steady beat piped over noise cancelling headphones, could make an amazing transformation in the way my students would respond to sessions. Research tells us that classical music reorganizes neurological patterns in the brain, and that when this type of music is used with a clear purpose the person can mentally and physically calm down. "Listening to music regularly clearly helps our neurons stay active and alive and our synapses intact. Listening to the right music does appear to facilitate learning and participating more fully in music making appears to provide additional cerebral advantages. Further, some music supports hemispheric synchronization, offering the opportunity to achieve brain coherence and significantly improves learning." (Bennett, 2009) I usually allow the students to work on a fine motor task while they are listening to the music, allowing them to really focus while improving and settling their brain patterns and allowing them to better function in a low stress environment.

For classroom teachers, I discovered research that suggests that there are two tasks that can be done interchangeably to change the entire mood in your classroom. The first one involves taking a walk. We have all seen the studies on the number of hours kids are spending indoors and in front of various media sources. This is time that used to be spent outside; running and biking and exercising. As kids spend more and more time inside and in front of media, not only do their bodies crave the exercise they need to grow and flourish, but they are loosing important nutrients from a lack of exposure to the sunlight. Taking them outside for as little as 10 minutes and having everyone go for a walk will expose their bodies to the sunlight and allow them to use the vitamins in the foods they are eating. Some classrooms teachers have decided that, on any day with decent weather, they will begin every day with a 10 minute walk. The results have been astounding. They are reporting fewer instances of disruption and more on task learning from the majority of their students; even those who have been diagnosed as having ADD/ADHD. If the weather is bad, another way to start the day and leave behind all the stresses of home is to begin the day, for the entire class, using music therapy.

I now begin every session with my students using music therapy. They are given noise cancelling headphones to wear and classical music piping over them. They are also given their choice of hands on activity like building a lego set, coloring a tessellation picture or playing with clay. For the first few sessions, I set a time limit and let them know as time is getting close. After a few timed sessions, I allow them to determine when they are ready. Usually it does not take more than five minutes for their entire demeanor to change. You can watch their bodies physically relax. Then they take off the headphones and tell you they are done and ready to begin.

During one session, one of my students appeared agitated while the music was playing. As this was usually not the case, I sat back to watch and see what would happen. Finally, the student pulled off her headphones and looked at me. "This is not working, Mrs. Holland." I was surprised, but asked, "Why not?" She responded, "Listen to this." and pulled out the headphone wire and the two of us began listening to the song 'Flight of the Bumblebee' coming out of the computer. I laughed and told her I understood, changed the song and she got back down to the business of settling down.

Another student fought me at every session with the need for the music to be classical. With every session, he would ask me if he could use his own music rather than mine. I explained that he couldn't because of the way mine works in his brain. This student enjoyed playing a game called Animal Logic. At the end of one session, when we had a few minutes left over, I gave him his choice of activity. He chose Animal Logic and I allowed him to put on a piece of his music. After less than a minute, he cleared the board into the box. I looked at him and smiled. He looked back at me, sighed and said, "Yeah I know. Your music works better."

With an overwhelming neurological response to the pop music, he had found himself frustrated with a game he normally enjoyed after only a few seconds. It was a quick easy lesson. Time after time, I find kids who come in flustered and not responsive to training to be much more compliant and focused after just a few minutes of music therapy. The pairing of the classical music with a hands on activity gives the learner a focus and seems to increase the effectiveness of the music.

Studies have shown that classical music physically rearranges brain patterns. It has been found that even students with ADD/ADHD benefit from the simple task of turning on classical music. Allowing the students to listen takes the random firing patterns in the brain that occur with ADD/ADHD kids and physically changes them until they are close to normal. When I use it in my training sessions, I begin by setting the amount of time that the student spends with the music therapy. I watch the student for visual signs of relaxing, give them just a few more minutes and then turn off the music se we can get started. After several sessions, I begin to allow the student to set the amount of time the music part of the session lasts. They usually come in and pick an activity. They sit down and pick an activity. They grab the headphones and sit down and get started. The music comes on and they work for a few minutes. Usually, they kind of nod their head and take off the headphones when they are done and we get into the meat of the session.

Once we have completed this activity, I notice that the students are much more able to focus and attend to the task at hand and the learning we do is a lot more effective.

Chapter 11

Comprehension

A big part of reading is the ability to understand what you have read; comprehension. It is one skill to be able to sound out and say the words in front of you and another to be able to understand what you have read. Comprehending the material presented is a crucial building block to a successful education. Early in school, kids are asked to read passages and then given a set of questions to determine their ability to comprehend the information. Some assessments recommend that the information be read to the kids and then the questions asked to help determine if comprehension or reading level is affecting the outcome of the assessment. Especially for the younger learners, this does make the test results more accurate. If presented this way to older readers, it may also be a more accurate test of the level at which the material is comprehended rather than the level at which the person is reading.

Either way, what we are looking for is the ability to read material and remember what has been read. When I did this as a child, I usually didn't bother to read the passage. I would go to the questions underneath and read them. Then I would go up and find the answer in the passage relying on the vocabulary words in the question to guide me to the answers. When questions came up that asked me to make an inference or a prediction, I would be annoyed because that meant I actually had to read the passage. The same held true when it was time to answer questions for a test review or any other assignment. Somehow, I knew that the information that was deemed important was that which would be pointed out via the assignments I was given. As a college and graduate student, I found myself having to read the material and take notes all on my own. This was a switch from what I had learned to do as a school child, but I was able to adjust and remain successful.

These were the coping strategies I employed to allow me to be a successful student. Not every student is capable of doing this on their own. Some have more trouble coming up with strategies for success. They are faced with new learning situations and don't know how to even proceed. When studying, they read over material and are then unsure of what to do with what they have read. The material, in large quantities is impossible to remember and gets lost in the confusion of the auditory or visual processing issues, short term memory struggles or executive function loss.

There are a couple of things needed to help those who struggle with comprehension. If a student is taught strategies their level of success is increased. They can be given short stories with questions under them, then taught to read over the questions so their brain cues on to key words or passages when they read. Once they have done that, they can read the passage through. Once they have answered the questions they remember, they should reread those they don't and skim the material to find the answers.

Another way to help work on comprehension is to either read a passage to the learner or have them read it on their own and ask a question or two to check for general comprehension. Then put the piece away. After about 10 minutes of session work, pull the piece out again and ask questions more in depth questions to check for memory and comprehension. A good source for short stories and questions can be found at www.superteacherwork sheets.com

When using pieces of writing as part of the training program, it is important to give a few minutes between the reading of the piece and when the questions are asked. This is important to allow the learner to clarify and synthesize the information that they need to. Then put the piece away and move to another part of the session. After some time has gone by, take the piece back out and ask the comprehension questions. If necessary, refer back to the piece. Ask them to find the answers they don't remember. Go ahead and point out to look for key words to help find the information they need. Train them to succeed.

In the classroom, it is helpful if the teacher presents the new terms before the unit begins. A pre-introduction gives the new vocabulary a place to go when they learn about it. For example, if you have never heard of a proton before and you read a about it in a unit, your brain will not know where to attach the new word to. If the term is introduced before, when you read it or hear it, your brain will know it has heard the term before and have a place to file the information. Think about it like creating folders inside the brain. If you have all the files created, the new information can be put where it belongs and neatly filed away. Having a file to place the material in also makes it easier to retrieve when needed. It is similar to when we discussed to dendrites and neurons in the brain and forming them into trees with branches and trunks. Providing tools and strategies such as pre-introducing the terms encourages the healthy foundation in the brain needed to retain the information.

I firmly believe that somewhere around fourth grade, all students need to be taught how to take notes and study. We usually just start telling them to take notes and then wonder why they struggle. Study skills classes are usually begun in high school and even offered in college as a response to students having no idea what to do. As teachers, we should not assume that because they are old enough to take notes, they will know what to do.

I also highly encourage students to learn to make and take notes using graphic organizers. Graphic organizers allow the student to take notes, group them in ways that appeal to them and make more sense of them. Take, for example, a spider diagram. (figure 11.1) Organizing the notes on the different legs of the spider groups the information visually. Think of it as helping to form the tree trunk and branches on paper to help it get into the brain correctly.

Utilizing a diagram, such as this, as opposed to just taking straight notes gives the person a visual cue as well as the auditory from the lecture and the kinesthetic from writing. Grouping the information together provides a picture in the mind and allows it to more easily be retrieved in manageable pieces. It also makes studying easier since the information is grouped together automatically in a way that makes sense to the learner. Once a diagram is developed, some students like to further visually break the information up using some sort of color coding. I have also found color coding useful even when taking notes on note cards. Some of my students will use varied colors of highlighter pens to record the information and some will use various color coded note cards. This simple task provides a very necessary visual break in the information and makes it less likely to run together, making it easier to retrieve the information.

Another form of graphic organizer that is highly effective is a Venn diagram. (Figure 11.2) The Venn diagram is most often used to visually show where items are similar and different. Items are listed in each box. The characteristics that make the things different are in the separate sides of the circles. Areas where they have similar characteristics are written in the parts of the circle that overlap. Venn diagrams are useful for a number of different types of studies, such as comparing different versions of the same story or comparing characters. In science, they are used to compare properties of different items being studied with the overlapping areas showing where the properties fit together. Once again, the pictorial version makes it easier to cement the information in our minds and allows us to hear and see what we need to know.

Another type of organizing information that many students find helpful is one that employs a two column method (figure 11.3). In the first column, the teacher or the student writes down a question that they expect to find answers for. In the second column, the student writes down the answer in his or her own words. The teacher is able to establish the concepts that are

88

important. The student is encouraged to synthesize the information by putting into his own words. Then the concepts can be further developed and built upon with vocabulary terms etc.

Figure 11.1 Spider Diagram

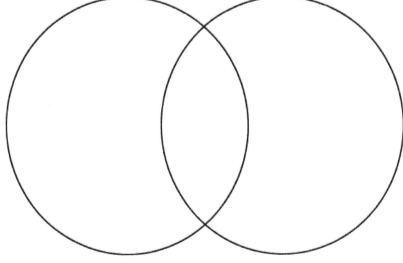

Detail

Main Idea

Topic
Concept
Theme

Figure 11.2 (Venn Diagram)

Figure 11.3 Question and Answer Note Taking

Question	Answer

Chapter 12

Short Term Memory

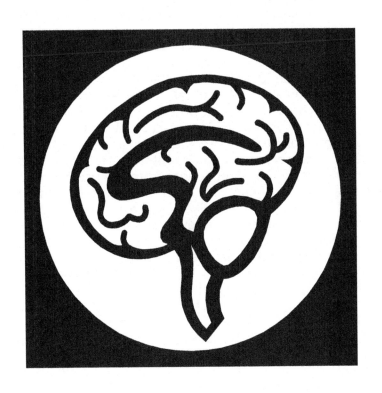

As noted earlier in the book, short term memory seems to be a consistent difficulty for those with learning disabilities. Fortunately, it is also an area that can be worked on with good results being obtained and coping skills can be established. It is also a skill necessary for success in life and in school. It is for this reason that we work on both ways to increase short term memory and develop coping skills for when it fails us.

You have probably met people who struggle with short term memory. As adults, they ask for a pen when given a piece of information they need to remember, such as an address or phone number. They are the ones with sticky notes all over their work space and to do lists posted everywhere. They are also the people you know you will have to call to remind a week before, a day before, an hour before and when you are leaving. Kids can be taught from a young age to practice skills to increase their short term memory to prepare them for success. When taught early, they become part of their routines. It is not just those with learning disabilities who benefit from the use of these skills, but every student. Those who successfully establish short term memory strategies are more likely to be successful throughout their entire school careers and beyond.

Short term memory skills affect people at home, school and work. Earlier in the book, we discussed the stress reaction in the brain. It was the research into this stress reaction that changed the way I deal with my family members and students. Let's look at a common situation. Your child is supposed to do the dishes every night. To be complete, the child is supposed to empty the dishwasher, load the dishwasher, wash the counter, sink and stove, sweep the floor and empty the trash. Despite the child doing the chore for years, there always is one part of the chore that is undone. You have completed the chore with the child, advised the child when incomplete and tried a reward system that includes a weekly reward for completing the task. Too often, what happens is that the task and reward become extrinsic and the responsibility to police the completion level is the parents. We need to find ways to make sure that this is reversed.

As parents, we often get frustrated when our children do not complete the assigned task. We show that frustration through language, tone or body language and the stress level of the child increases. The increased stress level causes a biological response in the child that exacerbates the difficulties the child has with short term memory. Then the task does not get completed. The parent enters the room to check the work and responds with the frustrated response. The child once again has a biological re-

92

sponse with an increase of stress hormones and nothing you say or do sinks in and the cycle is repeated.

As parents and teachers, we have to change the motivation for completing the task. If the main reason the learner does or does not complete a task is to not get caught or to count on our reaction or lack of it, we have failed. Going back to the kitchen analogy, the child will learn to complete the task of cleaning only to a minimum standard. If they think you are in a good mood or know you won't be home, the task will not be complete. We have to put the responsibility and the reward in their hands. So, we need to put a chart on the wall of the kitchen and list each part of the chore individually. When the child says the chore is complete, we go into the kitchen and go immediately to the chart. Then we go over each task on the chart, asking them if they are done or not. (Is the table washed? Great, put a check there. Is the sink clean? Wonderful, put a check there. Has the floor been swept? No, no check there. Dishes.... Trash... So you missed one today, go ahead and sweep the floor and you can try again tomorrow. It might be easier if you check the chart yourself before you call me in. I would love to let you have your extra 15 minutes on the computer every night.) You aren't checking the tasks to insure completion, they are. You aren't making the check marks, they are. You don't have to even go over the parts to be completed, the list is. This allows them to start to take responsibility for the earning of the reward. It becomes intrinsic and relieves the stress.

Put yourself in the learners' shoes for a minute. Imagine every second of every day where you have to play catch up. You haven't understood the lectures, have missed assignments and feel left out from classmates discussions when they are making plans between classes. You arrived at two classes unprepared and didn't know anything about one assignment that was due. And to top it all off, the noise on the bus was so loud that you missed your stop the night before and you are worried it will happen again. While this may sound extreme, these are truths for students who have short term memory issues that impede both learning and listening. They can also affect mood and self esteem. If you never know what your friends are up to, you may start to feel left out. If you are smart, but always arrive unprepared, you feel unorganized. If you didn't even know about assignments that were due, your grades suffer and you might give up. So we begin by giving them coping skills.

It is important to learn each student and their unique habits. Most are very tech savvy which makes keeping track of their life easy. Since most schools are getting better about accepting electronics as a reality in the lives of their students, many just need to learn how to use their phones features in a positive way. There are various planners available to download on any device. These planners can be used to not only to keep track of the assignments, but can keep track of the pre-assignments too. Some of the trackers have alarms that can be set to remind of the due date 24 hours in advance. Another tool, useful to most is the calendar feature. Calendars can be used to keep track of assignments, sports events, music lessons, practices, social events, changes of schedules and anything else that comes up in their lives. Even though this tool is on every electronic device they carry, I am often surprised at how few use it. They can make a note instantly on events as they come up. If details change, they can pull it up instantly and make those changes right away. As they move into adulthood, they can sync information up between devices and make sure they keep track of their activities, appointments and deadlines.

Assignment pads are handy for kids who are in schools that do not allow technology to be used in the classrooms. Even though they are readily used, they are underutilized. Work with your student to make sure it is filled out to the fullest extent possible. Current assignments should be written with enough detail so that they can easily get all the supplies they need to complete the assignment when they get home. They should also track the details of future assignments with a note made on the date the assignment is due as well as reminders in the book that break the assignment down and provide goals for project completion. Sticky notes can also be used in the assignment pad to help with reminders and deadlines.

One family I worked with was trying to figure out how to help their 12 year old son remember his morning routine. He would come downstairs every school morning and eat his breakfast. He put his bowl in the sink and then stand and looked to his mom, clueless as to what he needed to do next. His mothers prompting only seemed to leave him more and more frustrated. She could ask him to look at his feet and he still would not remember that he needed to go upstairs and get his shoes on. I suggested that mother and son make a list of the things he needed to do after he put his dishes in the sink. They made a list that said, put on shoes, brush your teeth and get your backpack and stuck it on the fridge. A week later, Mom reported that mornings had gotten easier after a short time because her son remember that he needed to go look at the fridge to get the remainder of his tasks. They also posted sticky notes in the bathroom and in his room to remind him what to do next. Another mother and daughter team made up a chart that could be used daily. The daughter could move a flower along the chart to make sure all the tasks were completed. Another of my students started making her own lists. During a session at her house, I found a sticky note list on her mirror that reminded her to comb her hair, brush her teeth and put on her makeup. Lists work and they work well for those who struggle with short term memory.

The most important part of working with short term memory games is accept that the more it is worked, the more consistent and successful the results will be. Pick several from the following list and suggestions and do something 5 days a week for best results.

Simon: I love this game. If you do an online search for free Simon game, you can find a great version that looks a lot like the original version. The best way to use this game is full sized on a smart board. When used this way it gives a visual cue, kinesthetic cue and an auditory cue. Remembering the ever complex puzzle requires the use of short term and working memory. Repeating the patterns with the whole body as required by using the entire smart board screen encourages the vestibular system. Whether done on a tablet or computer or smart board, the game Simon is one of my favorite online games for working the short term memory.

Concentration: I just use a regular deck of cards. For those who don't know the game, pick out a set number of pairs of cards from the deck. Shuffle the cards extremely well. Lay them on the table, face side down in evenly spaced rows. Each player takes turns flipping over two cards. If the two cards match, the player keeps them. If they don't, they immediately turn them back over in the exact same spot so the other players can try to find matches. The player with the most pairs at the end wins. This game is excellent for both visual and short term memory difficulties. We match up black 7's or red 3's. You can pick the number of pairs to pull out of the deck. I start with 10 pairs and increase it to 12 pair then 15 pair on the table at one time. This is a quick, easy and highly effective game.

UNO Cards: These games use the cards from the regular UNO game. Lay 15 or so cards face up in a line. Describe three cards from the line, not in order. When you are finished, have the learner pull them out of the row and place them in order on the table. (ex. Say, red 1, green 0, yellow 6. Pause and have the learner pull them out in order.) Once the student is comfortable with 3 cards, do 4 cards and then do 5 cards, making the brain work harder and harder and increasing the working and short term memory.

UNO Cards: Another game to play with UNO cards also involves the use of shapes. Use construction paper and make a large circle, a large triangle and a large rectangle. Place them on the table. Then place 15 number cards on the table face up. Give the learner two sets of directions and pause to allow them to complete the directions. (ex. Put the red 2 on the green triangle. Put the blue 6 on the red circle.) If the learner easily follows two directions, give three directions. You might want to write them down as it quickly gets hard to remember what you said.

Drawing: Draw a box on a piece of paper. Give the learner a set of directions. When done have them complete the directions. Give them as much time as needed to complete the task.

1. Color the front face of the box red. Put a star on the top of the box. Color it green. On the lower left hand corner write your initials in green.
2. Color the top of the box orange. Draw a pumpkin face on the front of the box. Color it purple. Draw cat ears on the top of the box.
3. Draw four wheels on the box to make it look like a wagon. Color the box green and the wheels blue. Draw a puppy in the box.
4. Color the top of the box blue. Put the number 1 under the front lower left hand corner of the box. Color the front of the box green.
5. Draw a line from the top to the bottom of the front of the box. Color the left hand part red. Color the right hand part blue.

You should have the idea by now. Just do one drawing in a session. You can draw other shapes, such as a prism or a circle and give similar directions.

20 Questions: This is a great game to play anywhere like at the dinner table or in the car on the way to practice. Pick an object like a rose. Then the person starts asking questions to try to guess the object. Is it alive? (yes) Does it breathe? (no) Does it have babies? (no) Is it a plant? (yes) etc. Keep track of the number of questions asked to determine a winner for the round.

This game actually works great for executive function and short term memory.

List It: This game involves remembering lists and giving your learner tips for how to more easily remember things. Give him the scenario and then the list of what is needed. Then remind your learner of the different tools he can use to help remember. Several types of strategies are given here. The child needs to not only develop the area of the brain that can listen to a list (or a set of directions) but to be able to come up with strategies to remember things on his own.

Here are the types of strategies that can be taught:

- Develop an acronym for the list. apples, butter, lettuce and eggs is a list you should be ABLE to remember. The acronym is made of the first letters of the items on the list.
- Chaining is a method of making up a sentence that contains all of the things you need to remember. Think My Dear Aunt Sally (muliplication, division, addition, subtraction) or Every Good Boy Does Fine (lines on a music staff).
- Rhyming all the things you need to remember is another tool that can help you remember the items on your list. For dinner, you are going to fix spaghetti. You need noodles, tomato paste, meat and bread. Think noodle-poodle, paste-waste, meat-feet, bread-red. Say the rhymes a few times to help solidify the information.

First Ten Presidents: (example of Chaining)	
George Washington	W-When
John Adams	A– a
Thomas Jefferson	j—joker
James Madison	m—makes
James Monroe	m—macaroni
John Quincy Adams	A—and
Andrew Jackson	J– juices
Martin VanBuren	V—vegetables
William Harrison	H—he
John Tyler	T—trumpets

13 Colonies (chaining)

Virginia	V-Very
Massachusetts	M– Many
New Hampshire	N– new
Maryland	M-Mommies
Connecticut	C– can
Rhode Island	R– Really
Delaware	D—dance
North Carolina	N– nightly
South Carolina	S—some
New Jersey	J– jiggle
New York	Y-yellow
Pennsylvania	P—peach
Georgia	G– gumbo

8 Planets (chaining)

Mercury	M-My
Venus	V– very
Earth	E-educated
Mars	M—mother
Jupiter	J—just
Saturn	M—made
Uranus	U– us
Neptune	N—nachos

Major Airport Codes (acronym)

LAX– Los Angeles California
MCI—Kansas City International
ORD—Chicago International Airport (O'Hare)
BOS—Logan International Airport (Boston)
MSP– Minneapolis/St. Paul International Airport
STL—Lambert International Airport (St. Louis)
JFK—New York, John F. Kennedy Airport
LGA—LaGuardia, New York
DFW– Dallas/Fort Worth
TPA– Tampa International Airport

Government Office Codes (acronym)

IRS—Internal Revenue Service
DOD—Department of Defense
NATO—North Atlantic Treaty Organization
NASA- National Aeronautics and Space Administration
DOT- Department of Transportation
CIA—Central Intelligence Agency
EPA—Environmental Protection Agency
FBI- Federal Bureau of Investigation
USAF—United States Air Force
USDA—United States Department of Agriculture

Texting (acronym)

AKA—also known as
QOTD- Quote of the Day
ROTFL—Rolling on the floor laughing
DUST- Did you see that?
HTH—Hope this helps
IGWS- It goes without saying
IBIWISI- I'll believe it when I see it.
ILMJ—I love my job
PNATTMBTC- Pay no attention to the man behind the curtain
POTUS- President of the United States

Visualizing: Another tool that can be taught, especially to those who learn well by seeing things, is called visualizing. Visualizing allows you to remember items on the list by creating a mental picture that contains all of the items you need. For your camping trip, you need: hammer, tent, firewood, and rain gear. Picture yourself setting up the tent in the woods in the rain. You have your rain gear on. Then imagine a cozy campsite with a nice wood fire burning.

Examples of Things to Practice Visualizing
- Things needed for a weekend trip
- Items needed to go on a campout
- Sports equipment needed for a game
- Items needed to take to a sleepover at a friends' house
- Pieces needed to bring to school for a project

Rhyming: Practice rhyming with any list of things your learner needs to remember for school or home. Half of the ease of re-membering the list comes with helping to create the lists. If you are a teacher, give the kids a chance to help create some rhymes for a list of items they will be tested on. For example, if your learner is studying for a test on the state capitals, she can be en-couraged to come up with a rhyming list on her own. Write down the list and make a game of remembering the items. This memory game is an opportunity to give the children several ways they can create coping skills for everyday tasks. Once they have gotten good at one or two of these techniques, find ways they can incorporate them into helping with routines. If your learner comes unprepared to class, encourage her to visualize the classroom while she is standing at her locker. What is she going to have on her desk? If she is missing things everyday for practice, encourage her to make up a rhyme that will help her to remember every day as she is getting ready.

Repeat It: This game is going to really work that connection and it is quite simple. We are going to start with three numbers. Give your learner a simple direction and then read each number separately. He is being encouraged to hear the individual pieces and hold them in his memory long enough to make sense of what they heard, then use the information to provide an answer.

If your learner is ready for the question, say it first. Then say each number separately. The learner should first give you the whole number and then the correct placement number. (Ex-ample: you say *the number in the tens position 1.... 6....... 9.* The correct answer would be 169 and 6.) Do these in sets of 10.

1. The number in the tens position. 4, 6, 8 (468 and 6)
2. The number in the hundreds position. 3, 5, 7 (357 and 3)
3. The number in the tens position. 1, 4, 8 (148 and 4)
4. The number in the ones position. 5, 3, 8 (538 and 8)
5. The number in the hundreds position. 5, 3, 5 (535 and 5)
6. The number in the ones position. 7, 4, 9 (749 and 9)
7. The number in the tens position 5, 6, 9 (569 and 6)
8. The number in the hundreds position. 2, 6, 4 (264 and 2)
9. The number in the ones position. 9, 5, 2 (952 and 2)
10. The number in the tens position. 6, 4, 2 (642 and 4)

1. The number in the tens position 7, 3, 5 (735 and 3)
2. The number in the ones position. 8, 4, 2 (842 and 2)
3. The number in the ones position. 2, 4, 6 (246 and 6)
4. The number in the hundreds position. 5, 3, 7 (537 and 5)

5. The number in the tens position. 7, 5, 9   (759 and 5)
6. The number in the hundreds position. 8, 3, 5 (835 and 8)
7. The number in the ones position. 1, 8, 9   (189 and 9)
8. The number in the tens position. 7, 4, 2 (742 and 4)
9. The number in the hundreds position. 4, 4, 5 (445 and 4)
10. The number in the tens position. 8, 6, 8   (868 and 6)

1. The number in the ones position. 8, 9, 8   (898 and 8)
2. The number in the tens position. 3, 6, 9   (369 and 6)
3. The number in the hundreds position. 9, 2, 7 (927 and 9)
4. The number in the hundreds position. 5, 3, 9 (539 and 5)
5. The number in the tens position. 5, 0, 4 (504 and 0)
6. The number in the ones position. 7, 2, 7 (727 and 7)
7. The number in the tens position. 8, 4, 0 (840 and 4)
8. The number in the hundreds position. 3, 7, 0 (370 and 3)
9. The number in the ones position 5, 8, 2 (582 and 2)
10. The number in the tens position 4, 9, 5 (495 and 9)

Repeat It! 4 Numbers: Please keep in mind the ability level of the person you are working with. If your learner is under 10, make sure he is capable of understanding place values up to the thousandths position. Do a few tests with just the numerals and make sure your learner can say the numbers. Then add the questions. Complete one set of 10 at a time.

1. The number in the tens position. 9,1,4,3 (9143 and 4)
2. The number in the hundredths position. 2,6,8,5 (2685 and 6)
3. The number in the ones position. 5,8,4,3 (5843 and 3)
4. The number in the thousandths position. 1,8,5,4 (1854 and 1)
5. The number in the hundredths position. 2,0,4,5 (2045 and 0)
6. The number in the tens position. 8,3,2,7 (8327 and 2)
7. The number in the thousandths position. 6,7,3,9 (6739 and 6)
8. The number in the ones position. 2,9,5,5 (2955 and 5)
9. The number in the thousandths position. 6,6,4,2 (6642 and 6)
10. The number in the ones position. 3,9,6,1 (3961 and 1)

1. The number in the hundredths position. 7,4,2,6 (7246 and 2)
2. The number in the ones position. 5,4,7,8 (5478 and 8)

3. The number in the tens position. 1,0,3,4 (1034 and 3)
4. The number in the thousandths position. 8,3,6,5 (8365 and 8)
5. The number in the tens position. 8,2,9,5 (8295 and 9)
6. The number in the hundredths position. 6,4,1,0 (6410 and 4)
7. The number in the ones position. 5,7,8,1 (5781 and 1)
8. The number in the thousandths position. 4,6,8,1 (4681 and 4)
9. The number in the hundredths position. 2,4,8,6 (2486 and 4)
10. The number in the tens position. 7,3,4,7 (7347 and 4)

1. The number in the thousandths position. 5,3,8,4 (5384 and 5)
2. The number in the hundredths position. 8,3,2,9 (8329 and 3)
3. The number in the ones position. 9,0,3,5 (9035 and 5)
4. The number in the hundredths position. 2,8,5,3 (2853 and 8)
5. The number in the tens position. 3,1,0,5 (3105 and 0)
6. The number in the thousandths position. 4,2,9,5 (4295 and 4)
7. The number in the tens position. 1,5,3,2 (1532 and 3)
8. The number in the ones position. 7,5,3,9 (7539 and 9)
9. The number in the tens position. 2,9,4,7 (2947 and 4)
10. The number in the ones position. 3,0,1,2 (3012 and 2)

Silly Statements: One of the ways in which people with auditory processing difficulties find themselves feeling like they are on the outside looking in has to do with hearing the details of conversation. Some report that they don't like talking on the phone because they have trouble following the conversation. Some report that in social situations they have difficulties hearing most of what goes on. It can be embarrassing for a younger child who really wants to participate in classroom discussions. He may hear one or two words of a discussion and raise his hand like all the other smart happy kids and give a completely out of context answer that gets him laughed at. These learners often develop social strategies to help them fit in.

The goal of this game is to encourage your learner to really listen to the details of what is being said. This game involves making statements that are ridiculous—but only by one word. Your learner will be encouraged to listen to what sounds wrong, identify it and come up with a word that makes the statement make sense. It will be a switch since they are used to trying to fill in where things didn't make sense. This game encourages the learner to listen for those details. You may have to encourage the learner to think about their fixes. (For example, if the silly statement is *I rode my cat to the store.* and she says *I took my cat to the store,* you may need to ask why they would take their cat to the store.) Then ask the question again. For some, coping skills may be very well developed and they may have to be guided through these exercises the first several times.

Do about 5 sentences at a time when playing this game.

1. The <u>cat</u> hopped into the bushes. (rabbit or bunny)
2. My favorite chore is <u>sweeping</u> the <u>dishes.</u> (washing or floor)
3. I grow spinach in my <u>bed</u>. (garden)
4. In the summer, I swim in the <u>road.</u> (pond, pool, ocean)
5. I sit quietly at my <u>tree house</u> while attendance is taken. (desk)

1. We eat lunch in the <u>bathroom</u>. (cafeteria)
2. He <u>painted</u> the baseball towards home plate. (threw)
3. The box turtle has a hard <u>mouth</u>. (shell)
4. A giraffe has a long <u>eye.</u> (neck)
5. The big, puffy <u>orange</u> clouds make pictures in the sky. (white)

1. Mr. and Mrs. Smith groom <u>skunks.</u> (dogs)
2. I brought my son to the <u>veterinarian</u> when he was sick. (doctor– although they could change son to dog)
3. On snow days, we build the tallest <u>mud pie</u> we can. (snowman)
4. Before the trains were invented, Americans all traveled by <u>engine</u> drawn carriages. (horse)
5. During the storm, the <u>dirt</u> swayed back and forth in the wind. (trees)

1. At night, the fan in my room squeaks loudly and keeps me <u>asleep</u>. (awake)
2. Andrew is eating a <u>tree.</u> (any food)
3. Chester flew a <u>bike</u> in the park. (kite)
4. Heather drove her <u>dog</u> to work. (car, truck, van, bike)
5. The baby <u>mice</u> flew from the nest. (birds)

1. Joe's truck has a flat <u>windshield.</u> (tire)
2. The cow didn't get enough <u>soda</u> to drink. (water)

3. Before you eat, always wash your <u>feet</u>. (hands)
4. The boy forgot his <u>pencil</u> for the baseball game. (ball, bat, glove)
5. I just love eating spaghetti for <u>breakfast.</u> (dinner/supper)

1. The <u>green</u> cat was hiding in the grass. (brown, black, white)
2. In the morning, I put my <u>shoes</u> on my head before I leave the house. (hat)
3. The little girl got a beautiful bouquet of <u>oranges</u> for her birthday. (flowers)
4. I enjoy wearing <u>necklaces</u> in my ears. (earrings)
5. In the spring, the grass turns <u>blue</u> when it warms up. (green)

1. The <u>penguins</u> in the trees at the zoo are very colorful. (parrots, birds, flowers)
2. I like going to the farm to milk the <u>chickens.</u> (cows)
3. The boy ate a red <u>crayon.</u> (apple)
4. I can't start the car until I find my <u>toys.</u> (keys)
5. When the <u>sun</u> goes by on the tracks, it blows the whistle loudly. (train)

1. The <u>fork</u> in my bedroom has a light bulb that is blown out. (chandelier, light, ceiling fan)
2. When we cut down the <u>flower</u> with the chainsaw, the sound was deafening. (tree)
3. When we go to the park, the kids really like to swing on the <u>slide</u>. (swings or they could change swing to slide)
4. The side door on our van <u>runs</u> open when you push a button. (slides)
5. Climbing <u>grass</u> all the way to the top is one of my favorite things to do. (trees)

Play on Words: This game encourages active listening, interpreting information, recall and processing. Because we also ask the learner to listen to information, hold onto it while they complete the task at hand and do something with it, we also work the short term memory.

In this exercise, your learner is asked to say a word. She is then given a direction involving changing the word into another word which she is then to say. (ex. Say football. Again without the foot.) It should be a fairly easy exercise and can be used as a warm up. Try one set of 10 per session. Alternate this game with Repeat It.

1. Say sunshine _ now without the sun (shine)
2. Say sad—now with an m (mad)
3. Say hat—now with a c (cat)
4. Say baseball—without the base (ball)
5. Say cannot—now without the not (can)
6. Say very—now with an m (merry)
7. Say wouldn't—now as two words (would not)
8. Say snowshoe—again without the snow (shoe)
9. Say would—now with a c (could)
10. Say spearmint—again without the spear (mint)

1. Say butterfly— again without the fly (butter)
2. Say didn't—now as two words (did not)
3. Say blew—now with gr (grew)
4. Say nowhere—now without the no (where)
5. Say I'm—now as two words (I am)
6. Say bowl—now start with a c (coal)
7. Say rattlesnake—now without the snake (rattle)
8. Say We've—now as two words. (we have)
9. Say boot—now with a sc (scoot)
10. Say eyeballs—now without the balls (eye)

1. Say popcorn. Don't pop it (corn)
2. Say they've. Now as two words (they have)
3. Say head. Say it again with a d. (dead)
4. Say toothpick. Say it again without the tooth. (pick)
5. Say that's. Now as two words. (that is)
6. Say fork. Say it again with a c. (cork)
7. Say hard. Now end with an m. (harm)
8. Say don't. Say it again as two words. (do not)
9. Say wasn't. Say it again as two words. (was not)
10. Say fun. Say it again with an s. (sun)

1. Say hamburger. Say it again without the burger. (ham)
2. Say weekend. Say it again without the end. (week)
3. Say aren't. Say it again as two words. (are not)
4. Say lotion. Say it again with an m. (motion)
5. Say we're. Say it again as two words. (we are)
6. Say wall. Now start the word with an st. (stall)
7. Say chair. Say it again with an h. (hair)
8. Say airplane. Say it again without the air. (plane)
9. Say shouldn't. Say it again as two words. (should not)
10. Say watchdog. Say it again without the dog. (watch)

Chapter 13

Executive Function

As I stated earlier, executive function is the ability to make a plan and follow through with it. For a student, this manifests itself in many ways. A simple example is of a student switching classes. Towards the end of the previous class, most students will have a quick thought process something like:

> Next hour is math class. I need my book, calculator, pencil, red pen, notebook and homework. I didn't have my folder last night, so homework is in my binder. So I need to grab my math folder and my binder and book. That will get me everything I need. There's the bell.

For a person with poor executive function, they will still be thinking, this is science class and it is Monday. Is it math next? This person will get to their locker thinking math and might grab their math book, but the binder and folder will be forgotten. Which means that the calculator and red pen or any other math specific items will be missing from their person when they sit down in their classroom at their desk. This is the student who is never prepared or it is the student who carries every item to every class, all the time so she doesn't forget something. These are the kids who constantly get points off for homework being late or being unprepared for class. In extreme cases, it is also the student who panics at the thought of going to the locker with all the other kids because they have gotten there so many times and been overwhelmed or panicked, that even the thought of going there causes them distress.

Executive Function Test: A simple test for the effectiveness of a person's executive function ability is one in which you think of a task that needs to be completed; making a bowl of cereal, for example. The person testing puts all the items needed for making a bowl of cereal in a container, along with several other items not needed. So along with cereal, bowl, spoon and milk, you might have a fork, plate, ice cream scoop, hairbrush, mirror, toothpaste and mixing bowl. The person with good skills will take the spoon, bowl, milk and cereal over to the table and sit down. The person with poor skills will grab the bowl and go over to the table. They might look to you for guidance or get back up and grab the cereal. They sit down and pour the cereal and look around. They get back up and come over and get the milk. After pouring the milk, they sit down and look lost for a minute before either asking you for a spoon or getting up one last time to get the spoon to sit down to eat.

Any task will do for this simple test as long as you have all the tools needed to complete the task as well as several not needed. You also need to make sure that completion of the task will be at a separate location so you can observe the steps the person takes to complete the task.

If the person struggles with executive function, there are several things you can do to help them develop their skills and tools you can help them to develop to cope with their difficulties.

Daily practice in defining the task at hand is very helpful. For example, if you tell them to get ready to go to the store. Follow that up with asking what do you need to do to get ready? Have them list for you what they need to do. This can be done with almost any task that requires several steps (example: set the table, clean your room, get ready for school) Having them verbalize the steps and helping them if they can't come up with all of them forces them to think about a plan before they start. Doing that on a consistent basis is an excellent way to develop the skill.

For a student, they should be encouraged to verbalize and make lists of what is needed. This can be done daily if necessary and written on sticky notes or on a magnetic white board that can be stuck to the inside of their locker or a combination of both. We have also attempted color coding notebooks etc for each class inside the locker to aid in determining what needs to be grabbed. The notes should be short and simple.

1st Math
Book
Green folder
Green notebook
Pencil bag with green duck tape

2nd Language Arts
Book
Blue folder
Blue notebook
Pencil bag with blue tape

Then sticky notes could be placed beside this list with special instructions (ex. Poster board for Language Arts) This helps the learner make a plan before they are in crisis mode when thinking becomes improbable or impossible. Working with the learners before they are in crisis mode will give them the tools they need to continue to learn to fend for him or her self.

As stated earlier, many schools require the use of specific assignment notebooks for all of their learners. It has been my experience that the proper full use of this tool is not taught. Teaching the students the proper use of this tool is an excellent way to help them learn to manage everything they need on their own. The list of supplies needed for each class can be written in this book instead of or in addition to what is written in their lockers. Notes about additional items can be written down in these books too. If the students are taught to date the notebooks ahead, they can begin to use them like a planner. They can go ahead two weeks and write down when they have an assignment due or a permission slip to turn in. Then at the end of the week they can make a note to remind themselves of what is coming up. Considering the high number of planners and even training classes on how to use planners available and necessary for adults, it is surprising we think that kids do not need them or the assumption that they will automatically know how to most effectively use them.

Games: When you think of games to use with those who struggle with executive function, think strategy. If the game requires the learner to make a plan to win, you are on the right track. An easy example of this is checkers. A person who does not take a few seconds before each to play to look at the board and come up with a plan will probably not be the winner at the end of the game. Chess is another classic game that requires the person to make a plan and follow through with that plan to win. Both games also require the player to make adjustments as they play to successfully win the game. Even games like basic UNO are more easily won if the players try to come up with a strategy to win the game.

Here are some other fantastic games for developing and challenging executive function skills:

Mancala
Chinese Checkers
Dominoes
Monopoly
Scrabble
Dungeons and Dragons type games
Poker or Blackjack

In the classroom or at home, set a schedule that includes a regular family night and games such as these to keep everyone on their toes and thinking. While you are doing that, you help develop their life skills and overcome difficulties.

Another way to work on executive function and memory is by memorizing things. Studies are being done everyday right now that look at the effects the digital age is having on the way our minds work. The effects are many and the changes are happening in the course of one generation, not several like we expect to see.

One of the areas suffering is our use of memory. We don't have to use our minds to memorize anymore. It used to be cumbersome to write a speech, memorize it and then make note cards that had just the high points on it. Now we can quickly scroll through the entire speech with the flick of a finger. Encyclopedias, dictionaries, phone books, maps and thesauruses were not exactly books that we used to carry around with us, but now a wide percentage of the population has all of those tools and more on their phones.

Need to look up a fact? It is easy enough to do with a quick internet search. Words can be spelled, phone numbers looked up and called are maps are spoken to us with a pleasant voice. We are not using our executive function or our memory very much at all and it shows in the way our brains are processing information. Kids are plugged in to electronics at an alarming rate too. The games they play provide instant gratification with more points and new levels. They don't have to memorize much except the quickest way through any given level. Our brains are changing quickly. So in this next section, I provide every level of memorization from the early learner with pre-language skills to the adult who just needs to sharpen their skills. Work on one piece at a time, until it is memorized, then work on the next. The list of pieces provided is definitely not inclusive or exclusive. Find what works for you based on what is important and interesting.

Memorize It-Nursery Rhymes for Early Learners

Nursery rhymes are the beginning of teaching language patterns and skills such as rhyming and rhythm that help your learner prepare to read. Collections of nursery rhymes are readily available. Read several every day. Start with rhymes that are just one or two stanzas long and, once one or two are memorized, add new ones. After a couple recitations, stop and let your learner fill in words. Leave more and more blanks until he has it memorized. Then move on to more difficult pieces one at a time.

It is important for your learner to be comfortable with memorization. Skills such as reciting the ABC's and counting to twenty can seem daunting to a child who is not familiar with memorizing. If we begin with tasks such as, "One, Two buckle my shoe..." the learner will already have a basis for the harder task of counting to ten.

Encouraging memorization in your young learner will make it easier to memorize pieces of information like multiplication tables, states and capitals and the Declaration of Independence.

Twinkle Twinkle

Twinkle Twinkle little star
How I wonder what you are.
Up above the world so high
Like a diamond in the sky

Twinkle twinkle little star
How I wonder what you are.

Little Bo Peep has lost her sheep
And doesn't know where to find them
Leave them alone
And they'll come home
Wagging their tails behind them.

Wee Willie Winkie
Runs through the town
Upstairs and downstairs
In his nightgown
Calling at the windows
Calling at the locks
Are the children in their beds?
For now it's eight o'clock.

Little Boy Blue
Come blow your horn
The sheep is in the mead-
ow
The cow is in the corn
But where is the boy
Who looks after the sheep?
He's under the haystack
Fast asleep.

Humpty Dumpty sat on a wall.
Humpty Dumpty had a great fall.
All the king's horsemen
And all the kings men
Couldn't put Humpty together again

Little Jack Horner
Sat in his corner
Eating his Christmas pie
He stuck in his thumb
And pulled out a plum
And said, "What a good boy am I."

Hey diddle diddle
The cat and the fiddle
The cow jumped over the
moon.
The little dog laughed
To see such sport
And the dish ran away
With the spoon.

Hickory dickory dock
The mouse ran up the
clock
The clock struck one
The mouse ran down
Hickory dickory dock.

Jack and Jill
Went up the hill
To fetch a pail of water
Jack fell down
And broke his crown
And Jill came tumbling after.

Little Miss Muffet
Sat on her tuffet
Eating her curds and whey
Along came a spider
Who sat down beside her
And frightened Miss Muffet
away.

Sing a song of sixpence, A pocket full of rye
Four-and-twenty blackbirds baked in a pie.
When the pie was opened the birds began to sing,
Wasn't that a dainty dish to set before the king?
The king was in his counting house,
counting out his money,
The queen was in the parlor
eating bread and honey.
The maid was in the garden,
Hanging out the clothes,
When down flew a blackbird
And snapped off her nose.

Memorize It: For Readers

The next pieces are divided into three levels, getting progressively more difficult. Start with a level one piece and then move up when you feel your learner is more prepared to move up.

You can pick if your learner will do better with a strictly auditory presentation of the material or if they would benefit from both an auditory and a visual presentation. Most will do better with both as it involves more senses.

Ideally, you should read over a passage for a couple of sessions. Then begin to encourage your learner to fill in blanks when you pause. Give your learner a copy to use between lessons and encourage her to read over the piece several times before the next lesson. Ask your learner at the next session if they know part of the piece and if she would like to say it on her own. As more pieces are memorized, mark them on a chart. Occasionally review and recite one of the pieces from the past to help build confidence. If pieces have been forgotten just fill in the blanks. Start with a level one and only progress up the levels if you feel your learner is capable.

Level One:

At the Zoo by William Thackeray

First I saw the white bear, then I saw the black;
Then I saw the camel with a hump upon his back;
Then I saw the grey wolf, with mutton in his maw;
Then I saw the wombat waddle in the straw;
Then I saw the elephant a-waving of his trunk;
Then I saw the monkeys-mercy, how unpleasantly they-smelt!

Beautiful by Socrates

Beautiful faces are they that wear
The light of a pleasant spirit there;
Beautiful hands are they that do
Deeds that are noble, good and true;
Beautiful feet are they that go
Swiftly to lighten another's woe.

A Time To Talk-by Robert Frost

When a friend calls to me from the road
And slows his horse to a meaning walk,
I don't stand still and look around
On all the hills I haven't hoed,
And shout from where I am, What is it?
No, not as there is time to talk.
I thrust my hoe in the mellow ground,
Blade-end up and five feet tall,
And plod: I go up to the stone wall
For a friendly visit.

The Arrow and the Song by Henry Longfellow

I shot an arrow into the air,
It fell to earth, I knew not where;
For, so swiftly it flew, the sight
Could not follow it in its flight.
I breathed a song into the air,
It fell to earth, I knew not where;
For who has sight so keen and strong,
That is can follow the flight of a song?
Long, long afterward, in an oak
I found the arrow, still unbroken;
And the song, from beginning to end,
I found again in the heart of a friend.

Work While You Work (McGuffey's Primer 1800's)
Work while you work,
Play while you play;
One thing each time,
That is the way.
All that you do,
Do with your might
Things done by halves
Are not done right.

Memorize It– Level 2 Pieces

Little Children author unknown
Little children, never give
Pain to things that feel and live,
Let the gentle robin come
For the crumbs you save at home;
As his meat you throw along
He'll repay you with a song.
Never hurt the timid hare
Peeping from her green grass lair,
Let her come and sport and play
On the lawn at the close of the day.
The little lark goes soaring high
To the bright windows of the sky,
Singing as it 'twere always spring,
And fluttering on an untired wing-
Oh! Let him sing his happy song,
Nor do these gentle creatures wrong.

The New Colossus by Emma Lazarus
Written for the Statue of Liberty
Not like the brazen giant of Greek fame,
With conquering limbs astride from land to land;
Here at our sea-washed, sunset gates shall stand
A mighty woman with a torch, whose flame
Is the imprisoned lightning, and her name
Mother of Exiles. From her beacon-hand
Glows world-wide welcome, her mild eyes command
The air-bridged harbor that twin cities frame.

Keep, ancient lands, your storied pomp!" cries she
With silent lips. Give me your tired, your poor,

Your huddled masses yearning to breathe free,
The wretched refuse of your teeming shore.
Send these, the homeless, tempest-tost to me.
I lift my lamp beside the golden door!

You Mustn't Quit—author unknown

When things go wrong, as they sometimes will,
When the road you're trudging seems all uphill,
When the funds are low and the debts are high
And you want to smile, but you have to sigh,
Rest! If you must but never quit.
Life is queer, with its twists and turns,
As every one of us sometimes learns,
And many a failure turns about
When he might have won if he'd stuck it out;
Stick to your task, though the pace seems slow-
You may succeed with one more blow.
Success is failure turned inside out -
The silver tint of the clouds of doubt -
And you never can tell how close you are,
It may be near when it seems afar;
So stick to the fight when you're hardest hit-
It's when things seem worst that you Mustn't quit.

America by Samuel Smith

My country 'tis of thee
Sweet land of liberty, of thee I sing
Land where my fathers died
Land of the Pilgrims' pride
From every mountainside, Let freedom ring
My native country—thee
Land of the noble free, thy name I love
I love thy rocks and rills
Thy woods and templed hills
My heart with rapture thrills, Like that above.
Our fathers' God to thee
Author of liberty, to thee we sing.
Long may our land be bright
With freedom's holy might, Great God, our King.

Memorize It: Level 3 Pieces

Excerpt from "I Have a Dream" by ML King Jr.
I have a dream that one day this nation will rise up and live out the true meaning of its creed: "We hold these truths to be self-evident, that all men are created equal."
I have a dream that one day on the red hills of Georgia, the sons of former slaves and the sons of former slave owners will be able to sit down together at the table of brotherhood. I have a dream that one day even the state of Mississippi, a state sweltering with the heat of injustice, sweltering with the heat of oppression, will be transformed into an oasis of freedom and justice.
I have a dream that my four little children will one day live in a nation where they will not be judged by the color of their skin but by the content of their character. I have a dream today!

The Gettysburg Address—Abraham Lincoln
Four score and seven years ago our fathers brought forth on this continent, a new nation, conceived in Liberty, and dedicated to the proposition that all men are created equal. Now we are engaged in a great civil war, testing whether that nation, or any nation so conceived and so dedicated, can long endure. We are met on a great battle-field of that war. We have come to dedicate a portion of that field, as a final resting place for those who here gave their lives that that nation might live. It is altogether fitting and proper that we should do this.
But, in a larger sense, we can not dedicate -- we can not consecrate -- we can not hallow -- this ground. The brave men, living and dead, who struggled here, have consecrated it, far above our poor power to add or detract. The world will little note, nor long remember what we say here, but it can never forget what they did here. It is for us the living, rather, to be dedicated here to the unfinished work which they who fought here have thus far so nobly advanced. It is rather for us to be here dedicated to the great task remaining before us --
-- that from these honored dead we take increased devotion to that cause for which they gave the last full measure of devotion -- that we here highly resolve that these dead shall not have died in vain -- that this nation, under God, shall have a new birth of freedom -- and that government of the people, by the people, for the people, shall not perish from the earth.

J.F. Kennedy Inaugural Address

In the long history of the world, only a few generations have been granted the role of defending freedom in its hour of maximum danger. I do not shrink from this responsibility -- I welcome it. I do not believe that any of us would exchange places with any other people or any other generation. The energy, the faith, the devotion which we bring to this endeavor will light our country and all who serve it. And the glow from that fire can truly light the world.

And so, my fellow Americans, ask not what your country can do for you; ask what you can do for your country.

My fellow citizens of the world, ask not what America will do for you, but what together we can do for the freedom of man.
Finally, whether you are citizens of America or citizens of the world, ask of us here the same high standards of strength and sacrifice which we ask of you. With a good conscience our only sure reward, with history the final judge of our deeds, let us go forth to lead the land we love, asking His blessing and His help, but knowing that here on earth God's work must truly be our own.

West Point Speech—General MacArthur

Duty, Honor, Country: Those three hallowed words reverently dictate what you ought to be, what you can be, what you will be. They are your rallying points: to build courage when courage seems to fail; to regain faith when there seems to be little cause for faith; to create hope when hope becomes forlorn. The unbelievers will say they are but words, but a slogan, but a flamboyant phrase. Every pedant, every demagogue, every cynic, every hypocrite, every troublemaker, and I am sorry to say, some others of an entirely different character, will try to downgrade them even to the extent of mockery and ridicule. But these are some of the things they do. They build your basic character. They mold you for your future roles as the custodians of the nation's defense. They make you strong enough to know when you are weak, and brave enough to face yourself when you are afraid. They teach you to be proud and unbending in honest failure, but humble and gentle in success; not to substitute words for actions, not to seek the path of comfort, but to face the stress and spur of difficulty and challenge; to learn to stand up in the storm but to have compassion on those who fall; to master yourself before you seek to master others; to have a heart that is clean, a

120

goal that is high; to learn to laugh, yet never forget how to weep; to reach into the future yet never neglect the past; to be serious yet never to take yourself too seriously; to be modest so that you will remember the simplicity of true greatness, the open mind of true wisdom, the meekness of true strength. They give you a temper of the will, a quality of the imagination, a vigor of the emotions, a freshness of the deep springs of life, a temperamental predominance of courage over timidity, of an appetite for adventure over love of ease. They create in your heart the sense of wonder, the unfailing hope of what next, and the joy and inspiration of life. They teach you in this way to be an officer and a gentleman.

Chapter 14

Auditory Training

For those learners who have been diagnosed as having auditory processing disorders, the following training is imperative to their success. Because those with auditory processing disorders have difficulties knowing what to do with the auditory cues they receive, we need to work that part of the brain on a regular basis. If it is not accustomed to listening to the variations in speech and separating sounds out from each other, being forced to do so with increasing difficulty will encourage the new connections to be made and will help the learner better those skills.

For the auditory training part of the program, we will focus on games and activities that will begin to encourage the brain to focus in on all the various sounds in words. These sounds, called phonemes, are the individual sounds in words. It does not necessarily correlate to a letter, but it can. For example, the word *dog* has three phonemes or sounds, /d/, /short o/ and /g/. The word wish also has three phonemes or sounds. They are /w/, /short i/ and /sh/.

Let's begin by looking at making you more comfortable with many of the individual sounds you will encounter in the English language. This is not a complete pronunciation guide, but it will help you get started.

Phoneme Pronunciation Guide

Key to the implementation of this program is making sure the brain can correctly hear and identify the individual letter sounds. Practicing the letter sounds will help aide both you and your learner in going through the program. You will feel more comfortable with the teaching process and will in turn help your learner feel more comfortable.

To learn the correct pronunciation of the letter sounds, first say the word on the list. Then say just the beginning letter sound. Say the word again and say the letter sound again, stretching out the word until you isolate the beginning sound. Practice each letter sound until you can isolate the sound of the individual letter easily. For example, say *b* and *big* several times until you are comfortable that the *b* sound is in isolation and there is nothing at the end (*b* instead of *buh*)

apple – short a – a	red - r
ache – long a – A	song - s
big –b	tiger - t
dog – d	up -short u
eskimo – short e – e	use – long U
Easter – long e – E	violet - v
fat – f	weasel - w
ghost –g	yellow - y
horse – h	zebra - z
icky – short I – I	shorts -sh
Ice – long I – I	child –ch
jump – j	kick – k
lamb – l	mouse – m
nose – n	octagon – short o – o
ocean – long o – O	penguin – p

Once you are comfortable with the sounds separately, you will be ready to work with the learner. In a typical session, you should play the phoneme switch game, the phoneme ID game, and the phoneme finder.

Phoneme Switch

The first game serves to start the brain listening for each individual sound. Remember that it is common for a person who has auditory processing difficulties to hear parts of words or parts of sentences. Then their brain attempts to fill in the blank spaces with a word or phrase they know. Unfortunately, they often fill in the wrong word or sound and they look at you with a confused look on their faces. In my house, this is a daily occurrence. I will say something like, "I went to the mall today and picked up some shorts." Whoever I was talking to will pause and look at me with a confused look. After a few seconds, I will hear, "Quarts of what?" My reaction is usually one of confusion while I try to figure out what they are talking about. It takes a moment for my brain to register 'shorts.... quarts' and then make the necessary correction.

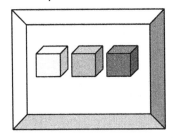

In this first game, the object is to give the learner a list of words that change only one phoneme at a time. The learner has to listen to the first word, then the second and determine which sound has changed and tap the corresponding block.

125

The setup can be very simple such as the one pictured here. Each block represents a different sound. Your learner listens to the words and picks up the block that corresponds to the sound that has changed.

For example, if the first word is *dog* and the second word is *hog*, the correct answer is to pick up or touch the first block. If the third word is *hot* the correct answer is to pick up or touch the last block. The next word might be *hat* in which the correct answer to the question is to pick up or touch the middle block. Do one list per lesson for each number of phonemes. Begin with one of the 3-sounds lists of words. As your learner becomes more comfortable, move to the 4-sound words; then 5. For some, this game is easy, especially before the background noise is added, for others, it takes more concentration. Watch your learner for signs of frustration to insure that the lesson is as effective as possible.

Phoneme Switch 3 sounds

List One	List Two	List Three
big	ran	pot
pig	run	hot
pin	pun	hut
pan	pen	cut
pen	pet	cat
den	met	cab
deck	mutt	dab
neck	gut	dad
nick	get	dud
pick	jet	duck
pack	jot	muck

List Four	List Five	List Six
dug	log	face
dull	dog	race
pull	doll	raid
pail	dull	red
rail	pull	bed
rack	puck	bead
back	peck	seed
buck	peg	said
luck	leg	sail
lack	log	rail
lad	lop	real

List Seven	List Eight	List Nine
seen	chief	dead
mean	cheese	bed
meat	geese	red
seat	gas	rid
sat	pass	hid
cat	peas	had
caught	peak	hat
bought	peal	cat
boss	pail	coat
bog	rail	code
hog	real	load

List Ten	List Eleven	List Twelve
get	hope	join
wet	rope	coin
web	rode	can
well	raid	ran
will	made	run
pill	make	gun
pail	bake	gain
rail	bait	gate
raid	bear	rate
red	care	wrote
wren	core	note

Phoneme Switch 4 sounds

List One	List Two	List Three
child	sand	plain
wild	send	plan
willed	sent	clan
build	rent	clad
filled	rest	clod
failed	best	clog
mailed	bust	blog
meld	rust	blob
melt	runt	slob
molt	bunt	slab
colt	bent	scab

127

List Four	List Five	List Six
slit	brain	lamp
slot	drain	lump
slate	drape	bump
plate	grape	hump
pleat	grain	hemp
plead	green	help
bleed	greed	whelp
blade	breed	weld
braid	bread	meld
grade	bled	mold
trade	blade	molt

List Seven	List Eight	List Nine
clack	plan	snap
click	clan	snack
flick	clean	slack
slick	cleat	black
stick	pleat	plaque
stack	plate	pluck
stuck	plain	cluck
stake	slain	click
stare	stain	flick
state	stone	fleck
skate	stoke	flack

List Ten	List Eleven	List Twelve
chart	build	corn
cart	built	cork
card	guilt	fork
guard	guild	ford
hard	gold	cord
heart	fold	card
harm	bold	cars
farm	bolt	bars
firm	belt	bark
perm	best	lark
perk	nest	lard

Phoneme Switch 5 sounds

List One	List Two	List Three
pants	dressed	firmer
rants	crest	former
runts	breast	farmer
bunts	blest	farms
bunks	blast	forms
banks	classed	forks
banked	clasp	corks
ranked	clamp	corked
ranks	clams	corded
rinks	claps	boarded
sinks	clips	boards

List Four	List Five	List Six
master	blend	stress
faster	bland	stretch
foster	blank	strep
roster	clank	strap
rooster	clunk	scrap
booster	clink	scram
boosted	blink	scream
busted	brink	stream
rusted	drink	street
dusted	drank	straight
dusty	crank	strut

Phoneme ID

When language develops in a child with normal hearing, sounds are easily differentiated by the brain. That is how we know the difference between the words *bog* and *dog*. The phonemes are easily heard and processed. For a child with a processing difficulty, these sounds can be muddled and very hard to differentiate between. Or, a child may hear the difference perfectly when in a quiet setting but not at all when there are other noises present.

The purpose of this game is to encourage the brain to hear the sounds individually and clearly and process the information quickly. It is very important that the phonemes are properly pronounced, so before beginning this game, please be sure to spend some time with the phoneme pronunciation guide on page 18. It may be helpful to have someone else listen to be sure the sounds are clear. For example, many people, when given a card that says *b* will say /buh/ - which is not correct. The correct sound is /b/ as in the first sound in *ball*. We do not say *buhawl*, we say *ball* and making the correct sound will help your child to correctly hear and identify. Some letters, such as *c*, do not have cards. This is because *c* does not have its own sound. The letter C makes either the *s* sound or the *k* sound.

This next game is based on the Denver Method Phonemic Training Program. The word lists and pronunciation guides provided are crucial to allow for parents/teachers to successfully implement this part of the program. (Katz, 2007)

First, introduce the sound with no prop. Say the sound several times with nothing covering your face. (/b/ /b/ /b/). Then say the sound with the key word. (/b/ as in the word ball) Then cover your mouth with something that will allow sound to penetrate, such as a picture frame with a piece of cloth in the opening. A piece of paper is not a good choice as it blocks sounds. Do the sound introduction again with the cloth in front of your face.

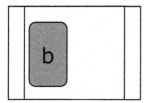

Then put the /b/ card on a piece of cloth on the table, like this. Introduce the sound a third time with the card on the table.

Your learner is instructed to touch the card every time the sound is heard. If they do not hear the sound, they are to tap off the cloth. Practice a few times and then introduce the words. For 'bad' he should tap the /b /. For 'happy' he should touch the table etc. Then take the /b/ card off the table and begin again with the next sound.

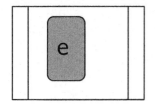

Introduce the next sound in the same manner. Have your learner tap either the letter card or the table. Go through all of the /short e/ words on the list. Remember that pronunciation is key to

your learner hearing the sounds better and more distinctly and the neural connections being made faster.

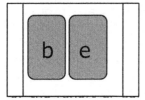

Now put out the cards for the first two phonemes. In this case it is the /b/ and the /short e/ and go through the word list for both letters. Your child should listen for either the /b/ sound or the /short e/ sound and tap either the letter he hears or the table if he doesn't hear either. Remove both cards and introduce the third letter sound in the same manner as the first two were introduced.

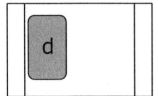

In this case, we have the /d/ phoneme being introduced. Go through all the words on the list specific to /d/.

Now put all three phoneme cards on the fabric. Your learner needs to listen to the words and tap either the /b/, the /short e/ or the /d/ sound. Introduce only three new sounds per lesson. Retraining the brain can not be done in one session, but will happen over time.

After the second lesson, a word list is provided that contains words with the first six sounds you and your learner has worked with. After the third lesson, there is a list that contains the first nine sounds and after the fourth lesson, there is a word list that contains 12 sounds. Continue to encourage the same pattern of either tapping the letter sound card when they identify the sound or off the fabric piece as they hear or do not hear the sounds in words. As you add the previous lessons sounds, remind your learner of each sound you will be working with in the same intro-ductory manner. After 12 sounds, start over again with three and add on top of those new sounds for the next three lessons. Please remember that the purpose is to train the brain to listen carefully for the sounds. As the brain learns to listen for individ-ual sounds, it will start to hear them more easily in spoken lan-guage as well.

Phoneme ID: Lesson 1

Make sure you are saying /d/ and not /duh/. For this sound, the lips should be apart as should the teeth, but only slightly. The tongue begins on the roof of the mouth and is released as the air is forced through. The /m/ sound should be made with your lips together. Be careful to not open your lips, or you will get a /meh/ sound.

The words either have a '+' or a '-' next to them. This is your key to help you, as the trainer, through the words.

Level 1

/d/	/short e/	/d/ or /short e/
+ mad	+ den	- little
+ dog	+ egg	+ played

- trouble
+ waddle
- plop

/m/
+ Monday
- plan
- nod
+ mop
+ clam

- list
- act
+ plenty

+ extra
- brat
+ breath

/d/ or /short e/ or /m/
   + duck
   - cow
   + chicken
   + mouse
   - horse
   - goose
   + deer
   + elk
   - beaver
   + moose

Phoneme ID: Lesson 2

Once again, please make sure the phonemes are being correctly pronounced. For the sound /b/, put your lips together before starting to make the sound. Open the lips and force the air out. Be sure to just make the sound /b/ and not /buh/. For the sound /short a/ open your mouth nice and wide before making the sound and it will sound more correct. For /n/, put your tongue behind the top teeth and your lips should look like they are smiling. It is OK when making the /n/ sound to release the tongue from the roof of the mouth just a little bit to make sure the sound can be heard.

/b/
+ bad
- happy
+ bell
- doll
+ elbow

/short a/
+ cat
+ apple
- bed
+ black
- tape

/b/ or /short a/
- drake
+ baby
- frog
- duck
+ latch

/n/
+ bean
+ need
- mop
+ penny
- calm

/b/, /short a/ or /n/
+ elbow
+ tap
- clog
+ penny
- pour

+ night
+ bottle
- whittle
+ patch
- mouse

Phoneme ID: Lesson 3

Remove all the cards and place on the fabric one at a time making the letter sound. Be sure you cover your mouth for each as you pronounce it. Three of the sounds are fresh in your learners mind but the other three have not been heard since the last session. The goal is to stretch the mind and build on prior learning. The letters are listed in parenthesis to help keep the exercise moving along. There are four words on the list that don't contain any sounds. Your learner should point off the fabric. This will not be easy at first, but should become easier as more lessons are done. The point is to retrain the brain.

/d/, /short e/, /m/, /b/, /short a/ or /n/

Block (b)	heed (d)
Peg (short e)	tiger (-)
Nut (n)	apple (short a)
Large (-)	pig (-)
Cat (short a)	mustard (m)
Stomach (m)	gecko (short e)
Doll (d)	bowl (b)
Phone (n)	four (-)

Phoneme ID: Lesson 4

As with the /b/ sound, be sure to begin with lips together. Forcing the lips apart is what forms the sound /p/. Be careful to not make it sound like /puh/. Say /p/ and the word penguin a few times alternating the word and sound to help you form the /p/ sound correctly. With the /short i/ sound, start with the lips apart and mouth open. With the /l/ sound, start with the tongue on the roof of your mouth, lips apart and mouth open before moving the air through. Stop the sound before moving your tongue. This will help make just the /l/ sound and not /la/.

/p/	/short i/	/p/ or /short i/
+ pass	+ igloo	+ silk
- bubble	- clog	- blog
+ pebble	+ litter	+ kelp
- best	+ slip	+ iguana
+ apple	- best	+ popcorn

/l/
+ long
- word
+ celery
+ bull
- refrigerator

/p/, /short i/ or /l/

+ inch	+ celery
+ ballet	+ guppy
+ kitten	- dice
+ pace	+ bowl
- bone	+ wasp

Phoneme ID: Lesson 5

This exercise will probably be frustrating because 9 different sounds are involved. Be sure to take a break and give a lot of positive reinforcement after this lesson whether it was done to 100% or 10%. Tell your learner his brain is going to work, but reassure him that he can do it. Explain that his brain is very comfortable where it is and that you are going to exercise it like you do your other muscles to make it work better. Then clear the board and reintroduce each phoneme individually, taking it off the board once it has been reviewed. Reviewing involves putting the card down, making the sound, making it again with your mouth covered and saying a word that begins with the sound. Once they have all been introduced, put all of the cards out and begin the list.

/d/, /short e/, /m/, /b/, /short a/, /n/, /p/, /short i/, /l/

Bow (b)	hobby (b)	best (b)
Act (a)	hair (-)	
Dog (d)	fat (a)	
Egg (e)	day (d)	
Tooth (-)	rest (e)	
Mom (m)	came (m)	
Nose (n)	knee (n)	
Pop (p)	pour (p)	
Icky (i)	toe (-)	
Lock (l)	skit (i)	

Phoneme ID: Lesson 6

The /t/ phoneme is started with the tongue between your teeth against the roof of the mouth. The sound is made as the tongue is moved. Make sure you just make the /t/ sound. For /s/ do not move any part of your mouth once you are ready to make the sound or /s/ will become /suh/.

/t/	/long e/	/t/ or /long e/
+ tent	+ zebra	+ needle
+ turkey	- blame	+ flat
- pole	+ tepee	+ eat
+ little	- coat	- ghost
- score	+ easel	+ knee

/s/	/t/, /long e/ or /s/	
- church	+ kite	- fan
- foggy	+ deer	+ sand
+ east	+ bit	- beep
+ super	- lamp	- pizza
+ clothes	+ sunrise	- shoe

Phoneme ID: Lesson 7

This exercise is difficult for any listener. Your learner needs to listen to the word, look at the 12 phonemes, find one that is in the word, find it on the sheet and point to it. This is where we really make that brain work. Reassure your learner before beginning that the goal is to make their ears and their brains talk better to each other. Clear the board and reintroduce each phoneme individually, taking it off the board once it has been reviewed. Reviewing involves putting the card down, making the sound, making it again with your mouth covered and saying a word that begins with the sound. Once they have all been introduced, put them all out and begin the list. There are no words in this list containing none of the phonemes. Make sure you tell your learner that every word they hear will have a sound on the sheet.

/short a/, /short e/, /short i/, /long e/, /d/, /m/, /b/, /n/, /p/, /l/, /t/, /s/

tug (t)	gecko (short e)	pop (p)
guess (s)	quack (short a)	glue (l)
lay (l)	fax (short a)	safe (s)
grape (p)	egg (short e)	take (t)
on (n)	wick (short i)	
bake (b)	weave (long e)	
my (m)	day (d)	
fade (d)	more (m)	
hear (long e)	cookbook (b)	
quick (shirt i)	fun (n)	

135

Phoneme ID: Lesson 8

The trickiest phoneme on this list is the /h/ sound. *H* starts in the stomach. The air pushes out of the stomach. The mouth should not move and there is no air going through the vocal cords. The whole sound is air.

/v/	/short o/	/v/ or /short o/
+ vest	+ dock	+ stop
+ savor	- tug	+ vine
- safe	+ knob	- nice
+ beaver	- hat	- face
- beef	+ got	+ smog

/h/	/v/, /short o/ or /h/	
+ habit	+ save	+ funhouse
- faucet	+ octopus	+ vocal
- locket	+bottle	- guess
+ horse	+ sock	+ perhaps
+ hot	- fun	+ raven

Phoneme ID: Lesson 9

/g/	/long o/	/g/ or /long o/
+ garbage	+ below	- pizza
- baby	+ open	+ soap
+ lego	- itch	- mud
+ egg	+ soldier	+ frog
- soap	+ soap	+ boat

/f/	/g/, /long o/ or /f/	
+goofy	+ roof	+ blow
- wish	+ garbage	- shirt
+ frog	+ orange	+ got
+ laugh	- cheese	- pizza
- thumb	- yes	+ freckles

Phoneme ID: Lesson 10

Remember to clear the sheet and introduce each sound individually. Think of it as giving the brain a little reminder of what is expected.

/v/, /short o/, /h/, /g/, /long o/ or /f/

Tug (g)	famous (f)
Live (v)	hairy (h)

Boat (long o)   shoot (-)
Perhaps (h)   very (v)
boss (short o)   food (f)
Such (-)   not (short o)
Eggs (g)   orange (long o)
Door (long O)   game (g)

Phoneme ID: Lesson 11

/k/	/short u/	/k/ or /short u/
+ cake	- earth	+ kangaroo
+ okay	+ ugly	+ pug
- city	+ pucker	- passive
- bite	+ doughnut	+ cake
+ book	- off	+ black

/r/	/k/, /short u/ or /r/	
- with	+ some	+ clock
+ write	+ candy	+ tugboat
+ green	+wrong	- best
+ glory	- piano	+ some
- blue	- tote	+ grade

Phoneme ID: Lesson 12

It is getting more difficult again. Hopefully, on this second go around with 9 phonemes, you will notice some slight improvements in the speed of the game. If not, hang in there, it will happen. Remember to clear the sheet and introduce each sound individually. Think of it as giving the brain a little reminder of what is expected.

/v/, /short o/, /h/, /g/, /long o/, /f/, /k/, /short u/ or /r/

live (v)	job (short o)	rat (r)
mayhem (h)	mutt (short u)	get (g)
alive (v)	nose (long o)	blink (k)
life (f)	flip (f)	not (short o)
hat (h)	lick (k)	gland (g)
up (short u)	stone (long o)	term (r)

Phoneme ID: Lesson 13

Two of these sounds need to be practiced. The first is the /j/ phoneme. As with /b/, it is very easy to put the /uh/ sound on the end and have the sound /juh/ come out. Be sure to just say /j/. Remember, it is not /juham/ it is just jam and it should

137

help. The /w/ phoneme is probably one of the most tricky to pronounce. We have always heard /wuh/. Say the word way and then make only the beginning sound. It was described to me as the sound a light saber might make. Make the sound several times before beginning this section of training.

/j/	/long i/	/j/ or /long i/
+ jello	- igloo	+ garbage
- gone	+ ice cream	+ fright
+ magic	+ rice	- lick
- kite	- open	+ orange
+ jump	+ sky	+ mice

/w/	/j/, /long i/ or /w/	
- fish	+ giraffe	- movie
+ wish	- horse	+ orange
+ coward	+ witch	+ island
- fan	+ high	+ how
+ bow	- train	- knit

Phoneme ID: Lesson 14

Can you hear the mission impossible theme playing? Get ready! It is time for the 6 minutes of hard, fast work that will make it all pay off, even though it hurts! You can do it. Hopefully, on this second go around with 12 phonemes, it will not seem as impossible as it did the first time. Remember to clear the sheet and introduce each sound individually. Think of it as the stretching exercises for the brain.

/v/, /short o/, /h/, /g/, /long o/, /f/, /k/, /short u/, /r/, /j/, /long i/ or /w/

move (v)	most (long o)
dare (r)	navel (v)
lake (k)	red (r)
doll (short o)	stubble (short u)
west (w)	fish (f)
page (j)	page (j)
nine (long i)	bust (short u)
pie (long i)	held (h)
wash (w)	pots (short o)
laugh (f)	stuck (k)
happy (h)	tone (long o)
game (g)	stag (g)

Phoneme ID: Lesson 15

The /oo/ of this list is made by forming your lips into an /o/ shape and slightly protruding your lips. It is not the sound the /ew/type sound in coo, but is the /oo/ sound in the middle of the word book. The sound is made with the mouth and chest and not in the head. The /ch/ sound is one that merits practice. The tongue starts out touching the top of the mouth and is slightly released to make the sound. The bottom lip is loose but slightly protruded, but the top lips are slightly tense. Think of the sound a train makes when making this sound and then stop at the beginning of the sound. For the /z/ sound, say the word buzz and freeze your mouth at the end.

/oo/	/ch/	/oo/ or /ch/
- oil	+ witch	+ cookbook
+ book	+ cheap	+ cheese
+shook	- this	- shout
- fright	+ church	+ teach
+ hook	- cool	-these

/z/	/oo/, /ch/ or /z/	
+ freeze	+shook	- shirt
+ zebra	+teacher	- babies
- pots	- lotion	+ chicken
- spots	+ close	+ sneeze
+peas	+ cheetah	+ smooth

Phoneme ID: Lesson 16

As with many of the other sounds, be careful not to put any extra sounds at the end of the /sh/ sound or you will end up saying shu. Just put your mouth in the correct placement and force the air out. Do not move your lips and you should have it. On the /long A/ sound, it is very hard to not say /ay/, although a little bit of /y/ sound comes out with the /a/ almost every time. You will know you are putting too much if your jaw starts to move when you make the sound.

/sh/	/long a/	/sh/ or /long a/
+shoe	- freak	+ labor
-base	+ acre	+ shop
+wish	+ cradle	- run
+ cushion	- coddle	+ rush
- cousin	+ obey	+ angel

/y/	/sh/, /long A/ or /y/	
+ yellow	+ plate	- water
-hello	+ squash	+ raisin
+ yolk	- where	- charge
- when	+ waste	+ young
+ yak	+ spy	+ trash

Phoneme Finder: Lesson 1

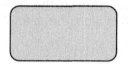  

The goal of level two is to further embed the sounds and to listen for them in context. Remember, the more we work with the brain to hear the individual sounds, the quicker the reception and processing should be.

To play, place three easily distinguishable blocks of color on the table. It can be as simple as placing three squares of cloth right next to each other on the table. The first square represents the sound being at the beginning of the word. The second is used if the sound is in the middle of the word and the third color will be used if the sound is at the end of the word. Place the target sound card at the top of the squares to help your learner keep it in his mind. Say the word and have your learner point to the correct square. Be sure to have him point as it adds an additional process to the game.

A 'b' next to the word is for beginning. An 'm' next to the word is for middle and an 'l' next to the word is for last.

/d/	/short e/	/m/
B– duck	B—egg	B—mad
L—mad	M—plenty	B—Monday
B—dog	B—extra	L—clam
B—den	L—chicken	M—blemish
L—nod	B—elk	B—moose
L—clad	M—dread	L—drum
L—waddle	L—Blitzen	M—damage
M- Monday	B—empty	L—germ
B—deer	M—den	M—wimpy

Phoneme Finder: Lesson 2

/b/	/short a/	/n/
bottle (B)	nasty (m)	penny (m)
hobo (m)	apple (b)	alien (l)
potato (-)	at (b)	clam (-)
wobble (m)	eat (-)	nurse (b)
knob (L)	ask (b)	mood (-)
dream (-)	creek (-)	apron (l)
balloon (b)	splash (m)	image (-)
cab (l)	quack (m)	funny (m)

Phoneme Finder: Lesson 3
(Corresponds with Lesson 4- Phoneme ID)

/p/	/short i/	/l/
pencil (b)	igloo (b)	girl (l)
bottle (-)	lap (-)	police (m)
apple (m)	brick (m)	pawn (-)
penguin (b)	begger (-)	learn (b)
tank (-)	inch (b)	green (-)
loop (l)	want (-)	dollar (m)
camp (l)	still (m)	onion (-)
trouble (-)	flung (-)	school (l)
apron (m)	flinch (m)	life (b)
scalp (l)	insect (b)	soap (-)

Phoneme Finder: Lesson 4
(Corresponds with Lesson 6- Phoneme ID)

/long e/	/t/	/s/
easel (b)	torpedo (b)	song (b)
pea (l)	best (l)	classy (m)
queen (m)	shelter (m)	black (-)
quit (-)	sheet (l)	glass (l)
ski (l)	doll (-)	sap (b)
seal (m)	habit (l)	bless (l)
tepee (m or l)	table (b)	pants (l)
eel (b)	lighthouse (m)	whisper (m)
bake (-)	baby (-)	zebra (-)

Phoneme Finder: Lesson 5
(Corresponds with Lesson 8- Phoneme ID)

/v/	/short o/	/h/
octave (l)	olive (b)	handsome (b)
wicker(-)	dog (m)	perhaps (m)
save (l)	onyx (b)	zebra (-)
violin (b)	dolphin (m)	hail (b)
fake (-)	flash (-)	funhouse (m)
beaver (m)	odd (b)	happen (b)
eve (l)	egg (-)	easel (-)
very (b)	ostrich (b)	habit (b)
blue (-)	doll (m)	short (-)

Phoneme Finder: Lesson 6
(Corresponds with lesson 9- Phoneme ID)

/g/	/long o/	/f/
garage (b)	orange (b)	frog (b)
dessert (-)	absent (-)	golf (l)
goblin (b)	gold (m)	give (-)
bag (l)	school (-)	effort (m)
north (-)	jello (l)	funny (b)
beggar (m)	only (b)	shall(-)
basketball (-)	walnuts (-)	myself (l)
gorilla (b)	nose (m)	that (-)
frog (l)	yellow (l)	guffaw (m)

Phoneme Finder: Lesson 7
(Corresponds with lesson 11- Phoneme ID)

/k/	/short u/	/r/
cake (l)	under (b)	learn (l)
okay (m)	doughnut (l)	ramble (b)
city (-)	otter (-)	door (l)
candy (b)	tug (m)	out (-)
worst (-)	ugly (b)	polar (l)
music (l)	mock (-)	sail (-)
pucker (m)	butter (m)	round (b)
best (-)	hush (m)	bored (m)
cage (b)	both (-)	child (-)

Phoneme Finder: Lesson 8
(Corresponds with Lesson 13- Phoneme ID)

/j/	/long i/	/w/
garage (l)	idea (b)	penguin (b)
jello (b)	lay (-)	cow (l)
zoo (-)	high (l)	wind (b)
angel (m)	five (m)	seven (-)
gorilla (-)	waist (-)	grass (-)
pigeon (m)	hello (-)	wash (b)
jack (b)	goodbye (l)	umbrella (-)
have (-)	idea (b)	arrow (l)
edge (l)	dinosaur (b)	however (m)

Phoneme Finder: Lesson 9
(Corresponds with Lesson 15-Phoneme ID)
There are only two sets for this list. The /oo/ sound is not at the beginning or end of words, so it is kind of pointless to do this exercise with the /oo/ digraph.

/ch/	/z/
choose (b)	zebra (b)
beach (l)	blast (-)
munching (m)	breeze (l)
show (-)	pizza (m)
archer (m)	song (-)
lunch (l)	hazard (m)
ash (-)	zoom (b)
chalk (b)	say (-)
shout (-)	buzz (l)

Phoneme Finder: Lesson 10
(Corresponds with Lesson 16-Phoneme ID)

/sh/	/long A/	/y/
sheet (b)	cradle (m)	loyal (m)
bars (-)	acre (b)	youth (b)
cashew (m)	these (-)	wet (-)
radish (l)	neigh (l)	backyard (m)
fashion (m)	flavor (m)	yet (b)
charge (-)	either(-)	chow (-)
rush (l)	obey (l)	young (b)
shark (b)	necktie (-)	beyond (m)
chair (-)	angel (b)	phone (-)

Now what?   The lessons are done and my child is not better. You are right.   Now is when the real work begins.   We need to begin adding the background noise. To accomplish this, I utilize youtube.   Do a quick search for hallway background noise.   In that list is a clip that is 5:37 minutes long. I find it to work well with auditory training. We turn on the clip and we start over again at the first lessons. Begin with the noise level low. I just use my computer and set the level at about 20%. We do several lessons with the noise at this level until the students feel comfortable and are mostly successful with it.   Then we increase the noise level by another 5% or10% and run through several more lessons at that level. We keep increasing the level in small increments until the level of the background noise is about equal to what it would sound like to listen to a person talking in a crowded hallway or cafeteria.

For my students Michaela and Rachel, introducing the background noise resulted in an enlightening and amusing situation. The two girls are quite competitive with each other, having been friends for quite some time. When we were meeting at the library, they came together and had back to back sessions. When Rachel came into the room, I warned her that we would be introducing background noise and that it would be harder than it had been. Rachel buckled down and we got to work. As we began to work, I watched Rachel's body language change. She was working as hard as she could to stay on task and it was showing with the way she sat up closer to the table, straightened her back and leaned forward.

Then I watched her form her hands into fists and by the time we were 2 ½ minutes into the training with background noise, her fists were hitting the table at the correct times. I could tell that the training with the constant background noise caused her to feel angry. She got through the exercises in about 6 ½ minutes and was clearly flustered. When we finished and I turned off the background noise, she gave me a dirty look and said, "I did not like that at all!"

Then when Michaela got in the room, I told her that we were going to do a task that she might find hard and that it had made Rachel angry. She looked at me and said, "Mrs. Holland, I am not going to get angry." I told her that we would see and that I knew it was going to be hard. We started the task. At about the 2 ½ minute point, Michaela looked up from the task and smiled. At 3 ½ minutes, she looked up again and said, "Mrs. Holland, I am not mad. But if that computer doesn't shut up, I am going to throw it through that wall!!" I laughed and we finished.

I tell you this story to let you know that it is hard on the learner and they do get frustrated. But in that first session with the noise added, we could go about to that 3 ½ minute mark before they would get frustrated. By the end of our time, we could about 10 minutes before that same level of frustration would set in. A ten minute attention span is a reasonable attention span. From there, we can teach them how to refocus and get back into what they need to be doing.

Once again, find and like Treating APD on Facebook to stay updated on further developments. I am working on an app that will allow the learner to play parts of these games through a computer program and I am hoping in a much more interesting way.

Brain Based Learning Techniques to Treat Processing Difficulties in the Pre-Reader or Early Reader

The testing for children under seven is still new and very hard to find. If there is a family history of processing difficulties and the symptoms are recognized in a child who is between 4-7 years old, these games will work. If your learner was fine at home, but at school seems to be excessively fidgety, unable to focus and not catching on quite as quickly as he should, these games are for you. Early intervention can actually change the way the brain reacts to auditory stimulus permanently, so if this works for your learner, the change may be permanent and life-long. No matter what, the brain training exercises provided will enhance the listening of your learner as the difficult task of trying to make sense of written language begins!

Remember, the goal of the program is to do more than learn the letters and sounds, but give the brain a new way to respond to those cues to help your learner become a more successful student. If the ears hear it and pass the information along to the brain correctly and quickly, your learner will be able to process and respond in an appropriate manner. When these skills are practiced over and over again, the connection will grow stronger and your learner will be more successful.

If your learner appears or has been diagnosed with a processing disorder, these tools were developed to work with your young learner by a mother and a teacher, and are meant to keep your learner engaged with the program and excited to use it. Movement and manipulatives are a part of almost every game in this program.

Spend about 20-30 minutes a day at least 3 days a week with this program.

Step 1:
Learn the Letters and Sounds

I don't think I can replicate the wonderful product put out by a company called Zoo-Phonics. Go to zoophonics.com and order their $38 parent starter kit. This program mixes letters with animals and sounds and is EXACTLY how a child needs to first be presented with the concept of a letter—which to them is a series of random lines on a paper— and the sound it makes. Be sure to include the movement aspect of learning the letters and sounds. Once your learner has the alphabet mastered on the letter cards, not the animal shape cards or the letter overlay cards, but just the letter cards, get this book out again. The rest of the games in this book are based on the concepts of letters and sounds that your child will easily master with the zoo phonics cards.

This picture was taken from the zoophonics website and shows three of the letters and how they are presented in three steps to the learner. It is just $38, but very well worth it.

When your child has mastered the letters and sounds on the alphabet cards, return to this workbook to continue training.

Everyday Life Practice:

On a daily basis, you can train the brain without the child even knowing what is happening. To do this, choose a time of day that is pretty routine and quiet around the house. For example, if your child usually plays in the next room while you are in the kitchen preparing dinner. Begin by holding a regular conversation with the child while not changing the routine at all. Stay in the next room and ask questions. The child will have to listen more attentively if he/she cannot see your face while talking to you. Continue your conversation for maybe five minutes. Do not be surprised if you have to repeat questions several times to get a proper response. For example, if you ask, "what are you playing with?" And your child answers "I'm building a tower." You should respond, "That's great. What are you playing with?"

Often, as parents, we find ourselves accepting the wrong answer, as long as we get one. We would probably usually peak around the corner, see the child playing with legos and go back to what we are doing. If, however, the child has auditory issues, what has actually happened is that the child has heard you ask a question and filled in some words where that he thought made sense and come up with an answer. If we accept the answer, even if it is wrong, we are not encouraging the child to listen better.

So by encouraging, but repeating the question until we get the right answer, we begin to encourage the child to be a better listener. Even better than the first response, would be: "That's great. Now listen to Mommy. What are you playing with?" With a pause in between the listen to Mommy and the question to allow the child to actively listen. If you notice that your child is beginning to answer the question correctly most of the time, add background noise that you control the volume of; like a radio in the kitchen. Begin with the noise at a very low level and slowly increase that level as your child seems to be able to hear you and responds correctly.

Training:
When we talk about training with a young child, we have to make sure that we remember that once stress is introduced, the level at which the child will successfully complete the tasks diminishes. So we have to make sure that we keep everything fun for the child. Consistency is also important. You might want to consider have a regular playtime when you play the learning games with your child.

Letter Trains

Letter Trains uses words that are three sounds. The game helps your learner to identify the sounds being heard and listen to their placement in a word. Each sound will be associated with a piece of the train. The beginning sound will be the engine.

The second sound, the boxcar and the ending sound the caboose. For example, if the word is 'cat'. Then the engine is 'c', the boxcar is 'a' and the caboose is the 't' sound. Say the word 'cat' several times. Then point to the engine, boxcar and caboose labeling each car with the corresponding sound. (ex. point to the engine and say 'c', point to the boxcar and say 'a' and point to the caboose and say 't'.) Ask your learner to point and say the sound with you. You may need to do several words before he understands what is being asked.

This game is intended for kids who are between 4 and 7 years of age. They have the concept of letters and sounds and are old enough to understand that the sounds can correspond to a piece of the train.

Don't start trying to play the game until he understands the part-sound coordination. Then tell your learner you are going to switch a sound in the words. You want him to put the block on the train to correspond to the sound you switch. If he gets it right, encourage him to take the train for a ride around the track. (ex. You would say, 'cat'. 'c', 'a' and 't' having them point. Then say the next word, 'mat'. Ask your learner which one changed? Help him put the block on the right car if he is having trouble. When the block is in the right place, let him drive it around the track.) Don't forget this is a learning game and if you have to 'help' a lot, it is fine. Do only one list per session and move on to another game.

Letter Trains

List One	List Two	List Three
Pop	Log	pig
Mop (engine)	Dog (engine)	Dig (engine)
Map (boxcar)	Doll (caboose)	Dish (caboose)
Sap (engine)	Dull (boxcar)	Dash (boxcar)
Sad (caboose)	Pull (engine)	Mash (engine)
Sack (caboose)	Puck (caboose)	Mat (caboose)
Sick (boxcar)	Peck (boxcar)	Met (boxcar)
Pick (engine)	Peg (caboose)	Bet (engine)
Puck (boxcar)	Leg (engine)	Bed (caboose)
Puff (caboose)	Log (boxcar)	Fed (engine)

List Four	**List Five**	**List Six**
Got	Will	Sun
Pot (engine)	Pill (engine)	Run (engine)
Pet (boxcar)	Pull (boxcar)	Ran (boxcar)
Pat (boxcar)	Push (caboose)	Rag (caboose)
Bat (engine)	Bush (engine)	Bag (engine)
Back (caboose)	Bash (boxcar)	Back (caboose)
Buck (boxcar)	Bad (caboose)	Buck (boxcar)
Bud (caboose)	Dad (engine)	Duck (engine)
Mud (engine)	Did (boxcar)	Deck (boxcar)
Mug (caboose)	Dig (caboose)	Den (caboose)

Goldilocks and the 3 Bears

Every pre-reader will need to figure out how the letter sounds fit into a word. For a child who with processing disorders, the sounds can get jumbled up. Simple and fun games that encourage the child to listen for specific sounds and figure out where those sounds occur will encourage connections to be made better and stronger. In this game, the three bears take the center stage. Give the learner as much help as needed at first and allow them to take over as they are able. For this game, it is not important for the child to identify the letter sound, but to learn to identify where the sound happens in the word.

Set Up: I found three stuffed bears and sewed Velcro patches on their bellies. Then I made gold buttons from yellow felt pieces with Velcro on one side. For a simple version, you could use colored in paper bears and yellow circles of paper. Lay out your three bears on the work surface. Papa is first, baby is in the middle and Momma Bear is last. Explain to your learner that you are going to listen to words and try to figure out which bear is carrying the sound with them; Papa bear if the sound is at the beginning of the word, Baby Bear if it is in the middle and Momma Bear if the sound is at the end. For each word, she is to place a gold button on the right bear. When the game is done, she can count to see which bear has the most buttons.

Goldilocks and the 3 Bears

'B' Words

Beginning	Middle	End
book	cabin	crab
bee	habit	slab
barn	marble	web
boot	trouble	lab

'C' Words

corn	bacon	pack
coat	chicken	brick
cat	focal	stick
carrot	tractor	quack

'D' Words

door	cider	mud
duck	older	bird
dollar	rider	slide
desk	model	sound

'F' Words

feet	different	stuff
frog	suffer	laugh
famous	guffaw	rough
February	coffee	tough

'G' Words

Beginning	Middle	End
gold	ugly	frog
grumpy	bagel	rug
gorgeous	begin	drag
green	finger	twig

'H' Words

happy	perhaps	hop
funhouse	ham	doghouse
hanger		

'short I' sounds

inch	pick
icky	chip
igloo	whisper
iguana	picnic

'long I' sounds

ice	nice	high
iron	bicycle	qualify
idea	triangle	horrify
iron	smile	deny

'j' sound

jolly	magic	badge
jump	digit	courage
jelly	banjo	fudge
jam	budget	midge

'L' sounds

long	balance	bell
laugh	melon	whistle
learn	villain	bulldog
love	yellow	willow

'm' sounds

Beginning	Middle	End
manatee	blemish	clam
mango	squeamish	time
middle	tomato	stem
mark	Clementine	phlegm

'n' sounds

nose	technology	moon
nut	benefit	balloon
night	finish	spoon
nice	spinner	clan

'short o' sounds

octopus	gone
honest	clock
honery	blob
omelet	prom

'long o' sounds

orange	throat	zero
own	goat	hero
open	float	throw
ocean	grown	ago

'p' sounds

penguin	Neptune	wasp
possible	apple	chirp
pretty	approve	soap
pacifier	apron	steep

'r' sounds

raccoon	berry	bear
rabbit	birch	color
racquet	diary	dollar
robin	apron	beeper

's' sounds

Beginning	Middle	End
scratch	castle	address
sheer	fossil	lettuce
saddle	session	erase
safety	possible	fence

't' sounds

Beginning	Middle	End
tricky	metal	racket
tired	pattern	wheat
terrible	pretend	admit
tacky	water	boat

'short u' sounds

ugly	blush
uncle	crust
untie	trust
underwear	nut

'long u' sounds

usual	amuse	cue
useless	music	review
unicorn	cube	rescue
uniform	huge	mew

'v' sounds

vine	tavern	brave
violet	reverent	cove
volcano	river	sleeve
vest	movie	receive

'w' sounds

water	between	snow
white	always	cow
wait	vowel	know
want	coworker	show

'z' sounds

Beginning	Middle	End
zebra	fuzzy	fuzz
zoo	pizza	fizz
zero	magazine	gaze
zipper	frozen	gauze

'ch' sounds

chunk	archer	punch
chilly	butcher	watch
chalk	lunchbox	search
child	teacher	beach

'sh' sounds

sheet	cushion	squash
share	fashion	trash
shamrock	pushup	radish
shallow	cashew	fish

Monster Mash

Establishing and understanding patterns is an important part of learning to read and make sense of written and spoken language. The goal of the game Monster Mash, is work on auditory discrimination. For the young learner, this is being able to hear the difference between the word red and rode. It works in a similar manner to the 3, 4 and 5 sound lists in Phoneme Switch for the readers. We are simply going to encourage your learner to listen for words that rhyme and respond when a word does not rhyme. When she hears a word that does not rhyme, she will throw a bean bag into the monster mash pot. At the end of the game, she can mix them all up and count how many words didn't rhyme.

To play, give your learner a bean bag. Then say the words on the list and have your learner repeat the words. When she hears a word that does not rhyme, she should throw her bean bag into the pot. Then give her a wooden spoon to stir the Monster Mash and pretend to eat it up before putting the game away.

Find a bucket of some sort. Ideally, you would use a cauldron that you can pick up around Halloween time in the decorations, but any large pot or bucket will work. Then you need some bean bags for your learner to throw into the pot. You can use a wooden spoon for the stir stick to make the game more fun and interactive for the learner. When you play this game, go through 2 or 3 lists in a session.

Rhyming Word Lists

bed	hat	dime	low
red	mat	rhyme	sow
head	bat	blame	mow
made	crate	time	rose
sped	cat	slime	dough
fed	fat	fame	below
spade	date	climb	ago
led	gnat	grime	snow
said	pat	lime	toes
dead	at	crime	throw

new	bare	look	blip
blue	air	book	clip
clue	care	spoon	dip
droop	rise	cook	clop
drew	dare	hook	flip
flew	fair	nook	hip
grew	stall	rook	slop
cruise	hair	balloon	lip
new	mare	took	nip
stew	pair	shook	slip

bead	bake	back	nail
deed	cake	lack	scale
bread	fake	broke	snail
freed	back	pack	small

greed	lake	rack	whale
lead	make	sack	email
had	rake	ache	hail
need	spoke	tack	take
read	stake	quack	tale
steed	take	attack	fail

baseball	band	cap	date
tall	stand	slap	plate
doll	state	map	met
bell	hand	upset	state
small	land	flap	mate
crawl	sand	wrap	create
fall	shot	strap	split
smell	demand	scrub	gate
call	understand	chap	wait
mall	bland	snap	straight

Head-Tummy-Toes

The game Head-Tummy-Toes places further emphasis on the rhythms of language. It helps us decode words if we can break them into parts. As adults, if we come across a new word (like a type of dinosaur in a children's book) we break it into syllables and sound it out to pronounce it. The next two games encourage the same idea. In this game, every word has three syllables. Begin by saying the whole word. Then verbally break it into syllables. On the third time, say each syllable and touch first our head, then our tummy, then our toes as the syllable is spoken. After the third syllable, stand back up and say the whole word. As your learner is comfortable with completing this task on his own, just say the word and have him break it into syllables on his own. When this game is mastered, move on to "Tap It Out" on the next page.

bi-cy-cle	tel-e-phone	app-e-tite
buff-a-lo	Sat-ur-day	li-ber-ty
di-no-saur	van-ish-ing	prop-er-ty
cur-i-ous	cam-er-a	dis-as-ter
ex-er-cise	De-cem-ber	reg-is-ter
fam-il-y	fin-ish-ing	med-i-um
e-lec-tric	la-dy-bug	ra-di-o
ex-ci-ting	o-ver-board	mu-si-cal
fa-vor-ite	gra-vi-ty	gas-o-line

in-dus-try   ham-bur-ger   Wash-ing-ton

per-i-od   gar-den-er   al-pha-bet

sub-sti-tute   vi-ta-min   won-der-ful

terr-i-ble   fam-il-y   por-cu-pine

for-get-ful   cus-to-mer   com-pu-ter

sep-tem-ber   af-ter-noon   cu-cum-ber

de-part-ment   fan-tas-tic   um-brell-a

car-pen-ter   lem-on-ade   can-ta-lope

pro-pell-er   bal-con-y   ad-ver-tise

Tap It Out

This game is for kids who are very comfortable with the Head Tummy Toes game on the previous page. Instead of every word having three syllables, these words have various numbers of syllables. This game helps focus on the syllables and makes a complex task easier to master. The purpose is to give your learner a concrete tool to help him master a difficult task. It may help immediately with a learner who is having difficulty with spelling. Give the learner a drum stick or other device to make this task fun. Then say the word. Have him repeat the word to check for comprehension and then have him tap the stick as he says each syllable and then say the word again.

air-plane   al-pha-bet   cal-en-dar

sun-shine   din-ner   por-cu-pine

va-ca-tion   won-der-ful   com-pu-ter

glo-bal   lap-top   fit-ness

De-cem-ber   en-er-gy   Wash-ing-ton

an-i-mal   an-y-thing   some-bo-dy

grand-fa-ther   com-e-dy   Jan-u-ary

com-pu-ter   ta-ble   pur-chase

un-der-stand   beau-ti-ful   sym-bol

cus-to-mer   ex-er-cise   tra-vel

ta-ble   sum-mer   con-firm

pic-ture   du-et   friend-ship

a-pple   class-room   qui-et

mu-sic   pen-cil   tea-cher

sci-ence   spe-lling   har-mon-i-ca

cam-er-a   im-poss-i-ble   op-er-a-tion

de-part-ment   pro-pell-er   el-e-va-tor

in-vi-ta-tion   wa-ter-mel-on   dis-cov-er-y

cu-cum-ber   cal-cu-la-tor   in-vi-ta-tion

cam-pus   con-ver-ti-ble   hu-mid-i-fi-er

mus-tang   dis-cov-er-y   dis-gust

Color Crazy

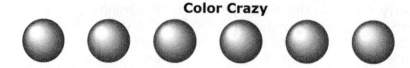

The goal of 'Color Crazy' is to improve auditory memory by following multistep directions. This game works auditory, visual, kinesthetic, vestibular and short term memory and is an excellent tool to have in your arsenal of tools. Your learner may be developing strategies to deal with his lack of processing ability. He might ask his teammates what the coach was saying in a huddle or ask the kid next to him which page he is supposed to turn to in his book. He may just copy what the other kids are doing during a game in PE. As the adults who are working with these kids, we want them to be able to lead and not always follow. Developing the learner's ability to listen to and react to multi-step directions is a good way to do that.

For this game, you will need two each of six different colors of circles. (think Twister board) For demonstration purposes, I used: red, yellow, green, blue, orange and purple. I cut out about a 10" circle out of cardstock and laminated them. Place them on the floor with enough room between them to allow for movement between the circles. The first sets of directions have two steps each. The third set has three steps. Then I have provided a list of action words that can be used for you to make up your own directions. This game tends to be a favorite as it does not seem to the kids that any learning is happening!

List of Action Words			
stand	swing	dance	stretch
whistle	clap	float	hide
jump	march	shake	flutter
hold	kneel	point	slide
hang	hug	leap	run
jog	scoot	skip	twirl

Color Crazy
Two Step Directions

1. Find a red circle and stomp on it three times.
2. Hop over to a yellow circle.
3. Jump from the yellow circle to a green circle
4. Pick up the green circle and put it on your head.

5. Twirl around three times and don't let the circle fall.
6. Put the green circle under your toes.
7. Get on your tummy and slither like a snake to a blue circle.
8. Stand up on the blue circle balancing on one foot.
9. Hop on one foot from the blue circle to the orange circle.
10. Put both feet on the orange circle and both hands on a purple circle.

Two Step Directions
1. Find a purple circle and run to it.
2. Leap from the circle to a green circle.
3. While marching on the green circle, whistle "O when the Saints"
4. Spin from the green circle to a red circle.
5. Hug the red circle and put it back down.
6. Jump to the blue circle and clap four times.
7. Jog to the yellow circle and do five laps around it.
8. Scoot from the yellow circle to an orange one.
9. Dance on the orange circle for 15 seconds.
10. Go back to the first circle and clap 10 times

Three Step Directions
1. Walk to a purple circle and whistle a song.
2. Kneel on the circle to the left and put your hand on the purple circle.
3. Jump up, stretch and point to a red circle.
4. Slide your feet to the red circle and hug it behind your back.
5. Place the red circle on top of a blue circle and shout out what color red and blue make together.
6. Put the red circle in your left and the blue in your right and run back to where you started.

Auditory Training: What's Next?

Now, it is time to add background noise. As you continue the lessons provided, add the component of background noise to the lessons to really begin the process of training the brain to *hear* better, especially as the ideal hearing setting diminishes.

As you do the phoneme section, turn on some noise. Begin with something that is as quiet as whispers in the back ground and increase the level about every three to four lessons. As you know, processing is the difficulty that people with APD face. They hear perfectly, but can't separate out the pieces of information. For some, the tones are all the same. For others, the sounds all come in at the same level. For all, processing the information, especially when there is more than one piece coming in at once is very difficult. If you go to youtube.com and search for background noise, you will find a clip that is long enough to accommodate several lessons. The one I use is under 'hallway background noise' and is a 5 minute clip.

You can download it to your computer or just play the clip while you are working. Begin with the volume at a low level so the brain can work into the idea. Think of it as getting ready to increase the intensity of the workout. When your learner seems to be able to handle the background noise, increase it a notch or two until the noise is at a level not unlike a cafeteria. Keep exercising at least three times a week and keep increasing the background noise as you go.

Chapter 15

Visual Discrimination

I have found two descriptions for those who have visual processing difficulties that I really like and that helped me begin to understand what it is like for those without an issue to cope in a school setting. The first was a demonstration piece I found on youtube where a teenager had asked to present to her teachers on what it was like to have a visual processing issue. She copied 6 worksheets onto overhead projector sheets. Then she took those sheets and put them on top of each other on the overhead projector and turned it on. Then she looked at her teachers and said simply, "Please read the first line of the 4th sheet." She remained standing there for about 5 seconds and said, "Are you paying attention? Please read the first line of the 4th sheet." She stood again for the five seconds and looked at the crowd, raised her voice and crossed her arms, looking exasperated and said, "If you would just pay attention" clicked her tongue in her mouth and turned back around. This visual example is very effective for those who need to 'see' something to understand. I have also found this to be a good way for people to imagine what it would be like to 'hear' every sound and have trouble filtering them out.

The second example I saw was a girl who also prepared a presentation for youtube. She took a pile of word cards, like a student who was preparing for a spelling bee would have, and threw them onto the table in front of her in a manner that caused them to scatter. She then looked up at the camera and politely said, "Read that page please." This demonstration is good for those who are trying to explain how words don't stay in place on the page when there are visual processing issues. Where auditory processing disorder makes it difficult for a child to listen in a classroom setting, dyslexia or visual processing disorders make it impossible. Think about the amount of information we are expected to take in through reading materials and taking notes and what it would be like to take that information in if the words, sentences and pages didn't stay in order.

When visual information is presented to the brain in this type of manner, we need to do things to teach the brain to look for specific pieces of information, and then we can begin to teach the brain to track that information in an orderly manner and make sense of it.

The following games will help a person who has difficulty processing visual cues and making sense of information presented visually.

Visual Discrimination

Remember when you were a kid and you went to the doctor's office. They always had the Highlights magazine on the table that had the hidden picture puzzle. If you were lucky enough to get hold of one that some kid hadn't circled all the pictures in already, it was a good way to pass the time until it was your turn. Those types of puzzles are actually very good for your eyes and brain. They encourage the brain to do a lot of visual discrimination as they look through the picture to find what they need. *I Spy* type books are another tool that achieves the same goal. They give you a list of things you need to find in a given picture. When you first start to do them, you will find that it takes more time. The more you do them, the more the pictures will almost seem to jump out at you. The *Where's Waldo* books are also good tools for developing visual discrimination. They can be a little more difficult than some of the others since they often have the same color and pattern repeated throughout the picture and what you are looking for is tiny, but they are a very effective tool. There are also apps that will show you a picture of an item and then show a search picture and time you on how long it takes you to find the item. Because these do not always keep the picture of the item you are looking for in front of you, they are another excellent tool that also works the short term memory along with visual discrimination.

Visual Perception

Our ability to make sense of what we see is our visual perception. Can we see the difference between the rise in the road in front of us and the grey of the skyline? How does our brain interpret the information it is seeing? Determining the level at which visual perception is developed in an individual can take several years. The person must be able to interpret what is being seen and then verbalize the concept to explain it. For example, a person might be having trouble determining where the edges of the stair treads are located. They may appear to be particularly clumsy as a youngster and may even avoid stairs; having hurt themselves on them too many times. It will not be until this child has quite an extensive vocabulary that she might be able to say something like, "I don't know why, but every time I try to go on the steps, the edges seem to move. I can't tell where my feet are and I get scared and fall." The type of concept development and language skills required to verbalize the problem happens long after the problem is causing issues. It is the same with the way in which a person, who is struggling to read can tell us. "No, I don't know what that word is. The first and the last things are both a circle and a line. I can't figure out what sound it says because it looks just like the other one." In reading, our visual perception is what tells most of our brains immediately which one is a 'd', a 'p', a 'q' or a 'b' without even thinking. Those that have difficulties with interpreting the visual cues given probably also struggling with reading.

To train the brain to look for those differences, we can do exercises and play games that encourage the skill. One such type of game to play for those who struggle with this are those in which there are several items listed or pictures shown. Only one item is different at all and it is by a small minute detail. (See Figure 14.1) You can find apps that achieve this goal. There are also online games and puzzle books that contain several puzzles like this. Another variation is to find games where the learner has to match up pairs that are visually very similar rather than finding the odd one out. (Figure 14.2)

Figure 14.1 Which one is different?

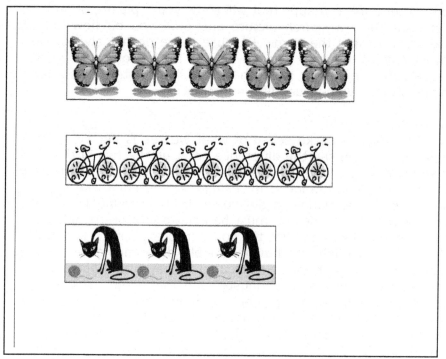

In Figure 14.1, each row of pictures is identical except one small detail. Find the figure in each row that is different. The attention to detail required for this game and others like it encourages the brain to look for the minute differences and differentiate between the items. It is the same attention to detail that allows us to see the difference between b, d, p and q.   In Matching (figure 14.2) the object of the game is to spot the difference and then find the item that has exactly the same difference.

Figure 14.2 Matching Pairs

The following game   Switcheroo (figure 14.3) is one I put together that can be used over and over again. You can change the rules as often as you want and work on any area you are struggling with. Use this game to work on short term memory, comprehension, processing and/or visual perception. Copy it, blow it up and put it on your fridge. Use it over and over again. One of my students' moms cut out several arrows which she lays out on the table and is using over and over again.

Figure 14.3 Switcheroo

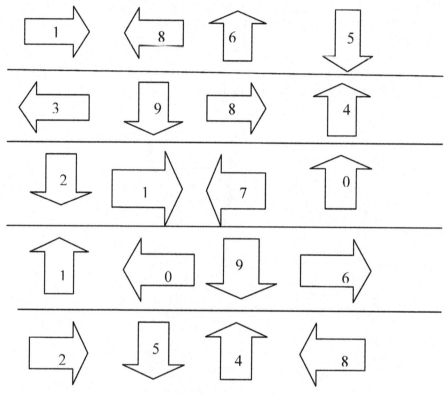

Read either the direction of the arrows (ie. Left, right, up, down, right...) or the numbers in each line (ie. 1,8,6,5,3 ...) until you can read it quickly. Then change the rules until you are comfortable again. Some examples of ways to change the game are:

- Read the direction of only the even numbered arrows.
- Pretend each of the odd numbered arrows have switched directions and read them.
- Add one to each number and read them again.
- Make up your own rules.

An additional use of this game is to establish a body movement for arrow direction. For example, for the up arrow, the person might be instructed to put both hands with palms up above their heads while raising one leg up resting the heel on the knee. For the down arrow, the learner can move both hands with palms down to the ground and shift the weight onto the heel. For left, the learner can move with the left knee bent, weight shifted to the left and both hands making a push movement towards the left. For the right, the weight shifts to the right and makes the push movement to the right.

The addition of a movement with the verbal directions is an excellent tool to increase processing and encourage sensory integration. You may want to begin by separating the two activities. Play the Switcheroo game. Then get out an individual arrow. The facilitator holds the arrow in different directions and the learner responds to the arrow. Have them say the words, "left, right, up, down" as they respond. Then try putting up a strip with several directional arrows. The learner should try to keep track of where they are on the line of arrows, say the direction and make the movement. When they are comfortable with both games, add them together.

To make the activity even more challenging, supply a beat and have the learner respond to the arrows to a beat. As their comfort level increases, so should the speed of the beat.

This is a very versatile and challenging activity. The possibility of including visual, auditory and kinesthetic variations and incorporating several senses at one time makes it a powerful tool to have in your treatment plan.

Visual Short Term Memory

To say that everyone learns and remembers things differently is a gross understatement, however there are pieces of information that are best obtained and remembered visually. For example, socially it is important to be able to see a person and recognize them. So being able to spot, recognize and remember the details of a person's face is a significant social skill. The information can be obtained through other means. We can run our hands over a person's face and have some indication of what that face might look like. We can be told to watch for a person with blue eyes and red hair. Those pieces of information can be put together into the beginning of a visual picture. If we touch the face, we have added kinesthetic information to those auditory cues and the picture becomes clearer (the soft smooth skin we felt coupled with the words red hair and blue eyes bring a certain look to our mind and gives us an even better picture.) We rely on our visual memory to help us get back to a spot we have been, identify our surroundings, find things we have put down, remember faces etc. We rely on our vision to help us remember all kinds of important things in our lives.

Personally, I am lean heavily towards being a visual person. I can have things described to me that get all jumbled up in my brain as I try to visualize what they are talking about. If I give or get directions, I am one of those annoying people who say things like, go to the McDonalds and turn right. Then go over both sets of railroad tracks to the first street where the laundromat is and turn right again. I don't know north or south and usually don't know the street names. I need to be able to see it to figure it out and remember it. For those who struggle with this skill, faces escape them as do landmarks and remembering where they placed a tool.

As with all of difficulties mentioned in this book, there are things we can do to begin to let our brain know these things are important. It is also the case that the more we tell the brain this, the harder it will work to make it easier to do what we are asking. The more we work out those connections, the more likely it is that they will be reinforced and that they will function well. Following are some pointers/activities for improving visual memory.

Memory: To play, I usually take a visual field, such as a rectangular piece of bright colored felt that you lay on a table. Then take 10 random objects and place them on the felt.

1. Have the person turn around and remove one or two objects. Then have them turn back around and tell you which objects you removed. Even better, have them return to the game 20 minutes later and identify the missing object. If they are having trouble remembering the pieces that were there, help them group the objects or find ways to remember what was there.
2. Another variation is to have them look at the objects for one minute then do another activity and come back to the game. Have them list the objects on paper and see how many they can remember.

Visual Closure
Visual closure refers to the ability to fill in missing pieces. You don't necessarily have to see the whole picture to know what it is. Think about a picture, like a dot to dot. Even though the pieces are not all there, the brain can often make sense of what it sees even with pieces missing. A popular internet example circulating is of the following paragraph:

Arocdnicg to rsceearch at Cmabrigde Uinervtisy, it deosn't mttaer in waht oredr the ltteers in a wrod are, the olny iprmoatnt tihng is taht the frist and lsat ltteer are in the rghit pcale. The rset can be a toatl mses and you can sitll

168

raed it wouthit pobelrm. Tihs is buseace the huamn mnid deos not raed ervey lteter by istlef, but the wrod as a wlohe.

If you remember back in the third chapter, I discussed that in normal conversation, a person will hear 7 out of every 8 sounds and the brain can fill in the one we missed so the conversation makes sense. A person with normal abilities to take in visual cures will do the same thing. Once we are successfully reading, we can look at a word and know what it is without sounding out every letter and thinking about every rule there is for reading that word. We glance at it and know what it is and as we read a sentence we see enough to read each word and have it make sense.

The game Missing Pieces (figure 14.4) encourages the brain to fill in the gaps in what we are seeing increasing a person's visual perception. For this game, you can make your own pieces taking out as much or as little of the word as you need by setting the font and the thickness, number and direction of the lines. For most, this game is not a challenge but for those who struggle, this is an easy way to work on developing the skill.

Figure 14.4 Missing Pieces

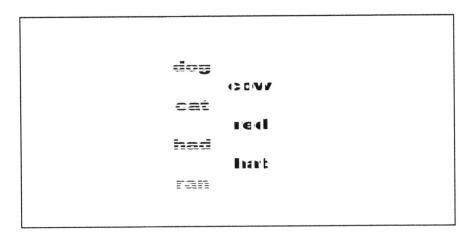

Finally, when we are talking about perception, the last area to look at is a person's ability to rotate objects his mind. It is what helps us tell the difference between b, p, q and d and make sense of the difference. It is also what helps with shapes and sizes and the orientation of objects. While some reversals of letters and numbers are normal, they should be gone by the time the child is in second grade. If not and if the child is also struggling with other reading, comprehending and writing activities, they might be struggling with this area. There are several games on the market to help develop this skill. They are puzzles that encourage the learner to fill in spaces with shapes that can be manipulated. There are also puzzles that show shapes in various forms and a picture that is missing one piece. The person solving the puzzle looks at all the objects, manipulates them in his/her mind and determines which one is the best fit. Regular puzzles are also great for developing this skill as are tanagram puzzles and games that can be found at most teacher supply stores.

The following sheet (Figure 14.5) is an example of one in which the learner tries to look at the word and then look at the variety of word shapes provided. The learner tries to see in his mind what the word would look like and then determines which shape best fits the word. You can make word shapes with various programs online. This sheet was simply created using the draw tool from MS word. Three different combinations of the word shapes are provided under the word. I did white out the lines between the shapes to make the task a little more difficult, but you can leave them if you would like.

Figure 14.5 Word Shapes

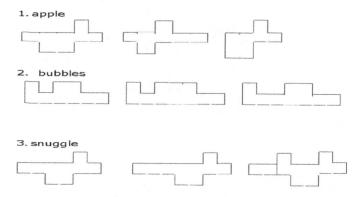

1. apple

2. bubbles

3. snuggle

Other games/activities that help with the ability to visually manipulate objects include puzzles. Having a **puzzle** out on the table that is age or ability appropriate on a regular basis is a good activity. Sit down to talk with the kids and work on a puzzle. Puzzles encourage you to look at a piece of a picture and then mentally manipulate pieces to figure out what will fill in the spot. There are games and puzzles that encourage you to pick the best option for what would complete the picture. An example of that type of game is included here as Figure 14.6.

The computer game/app **tetris** is a good one to play. The more advanced you get in the game, the faster the game moves and requires you to mentally manipulate the pieces. **Tanagram** pictures in the classroom are good tools to have as a game to play with. There are smart board/blackboard apps that encourage the learner to use the same skills too.

Using the Zoo Phonics cards outlined in Chapter 13 helps with this skill too. While the 'b', 'd', 'p' and 'q' are all lines with circles in different places that are hard to differentiate between, the characters Bubba Bear, DeeDee Dear, PeeWee Penguin and Queenie Quail look quite different and if the learner sees one of those characters overlaying the line and circle of the letter, they look quite different. When I do training sessions, I have found that even my older kids who struggle with this skill will use the Step 2 Zoo Phonics cards with the letters and animals overlapping as they go through the Phonics Exercises to help them to not have to think as hard as they process and quickly respond to the auditory ques.

Figure 14.6

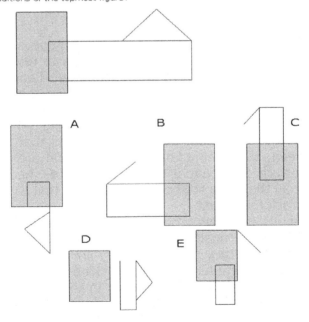

To which of these pictures could you add a single straight line to match the conditions of the topmost figure?

Visual Tracking and Saccades

At the beginning of this chapter, I described a presentation in which a girl was trying to explain what dyslexia was like for her. She took the pile of cards and threw them onto a table and then told the audience to read a particular sentence. For a person who struggles with this form of visual input, that is what reading is like.

I was called to meet with a mother and child. The child was nine and was reported to not be performing up to his abilities. He had received the diagnosis of auditory processing disorder.

He struggled with reading, comprehension and social studies in particular. We met in the children's room at a library. At one point, I asked him to go pick out any book he would like to read to me. He went over and picked out what appeared to be just over a picture book. He brought it over and sat down at the table. As soon as he started reading, I heard him really struggle with the words, even though it was a 1st to 2nd grade level reader. Within a few words, I grabbed pieces of paper. First, I covered up the words underneath what he was reading. Then I covered up the words on top of what he was reading. Each cover up brought up an obvious increase in the speed and fluency of his reading. Then I tore off a piece of paper and showed him only the word he needed to read next and moved it along with what he was reading. The change was almost unbelievable. I asked Mom if anyone had ever thought or said he could have dyslexic tendencies.

Because the words jumped all over the page and his eyes jumped all over the page when he was trying to read, he struggled more than he should have to read fluently. I suggested that both Mom and teacher look into providing him a tool to cover what he was not reading to help him read more fluently. This child is having difficulty with his visual tracking skills. He can successfully read individual words, even words that are flashed up on a screen, but when it comes to words that are all together on a page or are on a page with a lot of pictures, he has trouble filtering out all the extra stuff on the page and that makes it hard for him to track the words.

Often, adults with this problem will find themselves putting a piece of paper underneath what they are reading to help them keep track of where they are in the story line. This is also a successful coping strategy for kids with tracking difficulties. For the child I was working with, the decrease in the visual stimulation allowed him to immediately improve his reading fluency.

An easy game to use to help develop this skill is to have the learner play **word find puzzles**. Start with easy puzzles that have fewer letters. As the learner feels more success, add more rows of letters and harder words to find. Encourage them to complete one puzzle every 3 or 4 days. There is an app for smart phones that has word find puzzles. The one I have on my phone is simply called Word Search. Other app games that encourage quick visual tracking are games such as Candy Crush or Jungle Jewels on Facebook that have the player try to make lines of at least three like items by switching pieces around.

Similar to visual tracking is visual saccades. (figures 14.7 and 14.8) Think about how your eyes have to work to visually skip from the end of one line in the text to the beginning of the next or how sometimes you look up at a picture and then back down at the text. Your eyes have to visually jump from one spot on the page to another. Their ability to do that successfully is called visual saccades. A person who struggles with this skill often finds themselves on the wrong line of text when reading and will use a piece of paper to go from one line to the next when reading.

Figure 14.7
Saccades for Kids

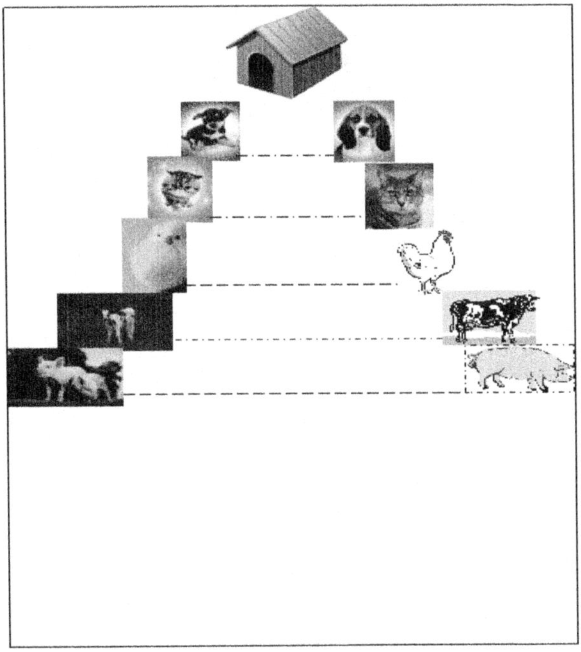

Figure 14.8
Visual Saccades for Learners

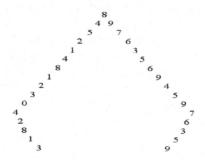

This sheet called visual saccades is an excellent tool to use to practice this skill. Have the person follow the lines across the sheets first (see 14.7 with lines.) Then, if they are successful, have them attempt the page that has the same shape and letters, but no lines. (see example 14.8) For more examples, see the data base links from the facebook page, Treating APD. Now, we are going to move to an activity that encourages the tracking saccades on a larger level. Tape two strips of letters starting at about 12 inches apart going vertically on an area like a door. Make the letters a size that the person can see comfortably at a distance of about 6 feet. Now begin to clap a beat. Have the person read the letters from the left and right, tracking across the blank space between the letters. The learner should not move their bodies at all when looking back and forth. Begin with the beat slow and increase the speed as the comfort level increases.

Another activity that works on focusing, tracking and saccades is to have a piece of paper with random letters printed in a 10 point font and another piece of paper with the same letters printed at the largest font you can print them (Figure 14.9). The person holds one piece of paper at arm's length. The paper should be at a distance where the person can easily focus on the individual letters. The paper on the wall should be at a distance that allows the learner to easily focus in on the letters and see them clearly. The trainer then says a letter to the learner then says a location. An example would be "C in your hand." The learner would then find the letter on the grid in their hand. When they have found the letter and focused in on it, they say "got it" and then find the same letter in the same position on the wall. When they have focused in on the letter on the wall, they

174

say "Got it" and the trainer moves on to another letter. To make it more difficult, the trainer can also tell the learner to name the letter in front of, in back of, above or below the named letter to make sure the learner is focusing and finding the letters correctly. Also included here is an example of a grid that contains pictures of animals (Figure 14.10) that can be used with pre-readers struggling with this task.

Figure 14.9 Tracking Exercise

Choose the grid that is the most age or interest appropriate for your learner. Then give your learner directions such as "Find the WA." When they have found it on the paper in their hand and it is in focus, they can say the words. Then say, "Go" and have them focus on the paper on the wall. Once again, when they have it, they should indicate that they do and you can begin a new sequence. For the animal grid, say a combination of animals, such as "chick- horse" and have them focus on one than the other. The object is to strengthen the eye muscles by working on the focusing repeatedly and often. In some places, the use of exercises such as these is being used rather than fitting the individual with glasses as these struggles increase with aging.

Figure 14.10 Tracking Exercise

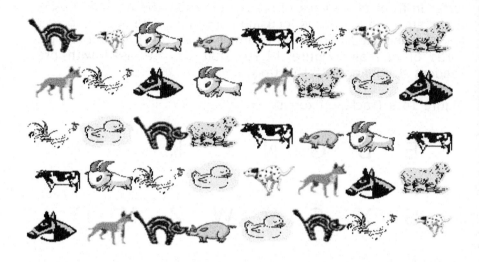

Some of the old fashioned video games are good for developing these skills too. The old video game pong and games like Pac Man are also very good games to play to improve tracking.

A side note: if you have a learner who seems to struggle with reading and has trouble with sports like baseball, kickball and soccer where they need to keep track of the ball as it comes towards them, this may also be indicative of trouble with visual tracking. Think about Charlie Brown always landing on the ground when Lucy moved the ball. If you are thinking of a person who seems to land on the ground all the time even if the ball isn't moved, you might have a person who has visual tracking difficulties.

Chapter 16

Vestibular and Proprioceptive

If you know what these are and how they relate to learning disabilities, congratulations! If you are like me about a year ago when I went to a seminar to have these concepts explained to me, this should put you ahead of the game a bit.

Have you ever spent an afternoon in a boat on the water? You got off the boat and stepped onto the dock and every sense you have seemed to be telling you that you were still on the boat and it was wavy. Maybe you didn't experience that feeling until you went to lie down in bed that night. Your vestibular system was responding to the overload of stimuli it received when you were on the boat. While you were rocking on those waves, your eyes, ears and proprioceptors told you what was going on and your body adjusted to doing what it was doing. You were able to relax on the boat without being assaulted by the sensory overload caused to your systems by the out of the ordinary movements you were experiencing. Then you got off the boat and your senses needed some time to readjust.

For most of us, our senses and our bodies are usually in alignment and while there might be times like: getting off a boat, getting up suddenly or being on an elevator, when our senses respond a few seconds after our bodies have stopped moving, for the most part our senses respond adequately so that we know where our bodies are in relation to the world around us. This is not the case for everyone. For some, that feeling of getting off the boat is an everyday occurrence. The signals between their eyes, ears and proprioceptors are always just a little off and they have trouble with sensory information.

Imagine if every time you stood up, you felt like you were falling over. Imagine if you had trouble gauging how close you were to the wall and were afraid of running into it. A child with difficulties with sensory information coming together is the child who, when walking in the line, has his hands on the wall and always seems to trip over the kid in front of him. He is the child who constantly picks at the tag of his shirt, can't stand the elastic around his coat and is bothered by the seam of his sock. For most people, those items might be a distraction for a few minutes while our senses adjust to the sensation. Our proprioceptors learn to ignore the input and it is forgotten. For others, that tag with the itchy corner is a constant irritation through out the day because their senses don't turn off the input.

So while some kids struggle with the auditory input and others struggle with the visual input, still others have their senses constantly barraged by the input not lining up. They are often on constant sensory overload. While one child in the classroom is trying to figure out why the words won't line up and another is

178

trying to find out the source of the noise she is hearing, a third child is trying to figure out what is stabbing them in the neck and while trying to find the source of the distraction feels like they are falling off their chair.

We all know people who are considered clumsy. By the time they are teenagers, they usually know who they are too. They are those who refer to themselves as an accident looking for a place to happen. They often do not play sports involving a great deal of coordination, knowing that they will be the team member on the sidelines in a cast. The proprioceptors don't always give them the information needed quickly enough for the response to be there to alert them to danger or if they do get the necessary information; their bodies don't respond as quickly as others.

As with the other disabilities discussed, these people often struggle with the same difficulties as those with other neurological struggles. The same good news also applies. We can train their brains to remember better, help them get their senses in line and work on the executive function. Here are some things to do to help.

VIDEO GAMES: Purchase a Wii. I know it sounds crazy to recommend video games, but the Wii type games encourage a great deal of coordination. Wii fit, tennis, all the Just Dance games, Guitar Hero and any other game that requires the body to get up and move in sync. When I discussed this with one of my students who struggles to coordinate and does not play sports as a result of his feelings of inadequacy, he stopped me and said, "Wait, just you just tell me to play Guitar Hero?" When I smiled and said that I had, he responded, "I've gotta call my Mom and you tell her, cause she's not gonna believe me." Games that require the whole body to move together to achieve a higher level or more points are great ways for the kids to improve coordination.

TWISTER/Bop It: Yes, the old floor game twister requires the person to coordinate body parts in an effort to stay balanced. It is an excellent training tool for the muscles and coordination. The series of games called Bop It give an audio cue that requires the body to respond in some way. It is an excellent tool to use to increase learning and coordination.

PLAY: Get them outside. Purchase a jump rope and teach them to use it. Make a hop scotch with chalk on the side walk and play with them. Find a local park with modern equipment in it. They often have been designed with thought given to utilizing the various muscle groups and coordinating their bodies. Even some of the older play structures are excellent, especially things like swings and merry go rounds. Think about the coordination required to go across a set of monkey bars. You have to use arms, legs and body together to move all the way across the span without falling.

YOGA: For those of you who are passionate about yoga, if your child struggles with coordination, get them involved. Yoga requires a great deal of coordination, is a wonderful strength building activity, does not involve competition and deals with activities that cross the midline.

BALANCE BEAM: I would not recommend starting with a balance beam that is 4 feet off the ground. I would recommend that you start with a tape line on the floor. Begin with having the person walk down the line with toes pointed inward (pigeon toed) all the way down the line. Then have them turn and walk with their toes pointed outward (duck walk) all the way down the line. You can also have them walk with one foot directly in front of the other, heel to toe down the line. Another activity is to have them crawl down the line. Crawling requires the person to cross the midline and use both sides of the brain at the same time.

Chapter 17

Activities

I have been asked by many people about putting kids with learning issues into band or foreign language classes. I always explain that those classes are not only necessary for kids, but can be extremely beneficial.

Last summer, I attended a program put on by a group called Sheltered Reality. I sat in the crowd listening and watching with my mind racing. The man at the head of the group talked to the crowd about why and how he started the group. He discussed the story of a young girl who was diagnosed as being dyslexic and how she was suffering emotionally and socially when she came to one of the practices. I keyed on instantly and began to watch and listen from way more than an audience member perspective.

Part of the appeal of the group is that, even though they now hold practices in 11 states, they are all taught the same music and the same moves. If a child practices in Missouri, but can't attend an upcoming performance in Missouri, they can do to a performance in Minnesota, set up and play in that concert without a missed beat and the beats are amazing. I watched kids bouncing balls off their drums to one side and catching the ball of the person next to them without missing a beat. They were using both sides of their brain, processing, following directions. It was amazing. If you go to YouTube and do a search for 'Sheltered Reality song with balls' and you will see the amazing things a brain can be taught to do. Take a few minutes to search around and watch more of their performances and think about the brain power and processing speed required to do the tasks being done.

For those who process information at a slower speed, for whatever reason, learning to read and play music is an activity that requires more processing, at a quicker speed with quicker reactions. Let's think for a minute about what must happen for a person to read and play music. First, a person must learn what the series of dots and lines they are seeing on a page mean. They must then learn how those lines and dots require their bodies to react to form the correct corresponding sound. Basic language is read on the left side of the brain. Music is interpreted on the right side of the brain which forces you to cross the midline to perform. This must be done in the space of a second to a part of a second, over and over again to be successful. If the person is a member of a group, they must also learn how what they are seeing and hearing interacts with those around them. With practice, all these things become second nature: the processing speed has increased as a result of forcing both sides of the rain to work together quickly.

182

The same is true of learning to speak a foreign language. From birth, kids are capable of learning and understanding more than one language. When we teach a foreign language, we encourage several things to happen. The brain hears words in a foreign language. Hearing and interpreting the clues is a left brain activity. Transposing that into either the primary language or into the foreign language happens on the right side of the brain. Those cues then have to be coordinated into a spoken response which activates yet another section of the brain. Done over and over again, the rate at which we process the information increases as our performance, in this case the ability to speak a foreign language, also increases.

If you are not fluent in a second language, do not despair. Programs that promote the acquisition of a second language are readily available. Find one that encourages interaction as this interaction is what will encourage the development of these new skills.

The following is a quick music lesson that will help you get started with learning this type of skill. I have included a drum lesson since that is an instrument that can be begun with very few materials and very little money, but any instrument will work to train that brain and the interests of the child should be considered. I have found that some students do not mind the loud sounds produced by an instrument like a drum or a trumpet, while the onslaught of a drum beat causes some to physically cringe. Likewise, some students are perfectly comfortable with the idea of a beginning band with all of the noise associated with many learning to play for the first time, while some are physically ill at the thought. For those who are more sensitive, a smaller group, private lessons or an orchestra class might be more appropriate.

As I stated earlier, I can only imagine what an orchestra must feel and sound like to my son Ben since he hears every sound around him with such clarity.

Activity: Get the Beat

Basic Music Lesson: In the simplest phrase of music, there are four beats. These beats can be said as four evenly spaced notes of rhythm. Much the same as a dollar is divided into four parts with quarters, these notes can be referred to as quarter notes and are most commonly spoken as a 'ta' phrase. One measure (phrase) of music is spoken as ta-ta-ta-ta. Each 'ta' can be broken in half and divided into two 'ti-ti' or eighth notes. So one measure can also be read, 'ti-ti, ti-ti, ti-ti, ti-ti'. Creating rhythms can be done using a combination of 'ta' and 'ti-ti' phrases. For this very simple lesson, we will also add a quarter rest. Just like the quarter note, there would be four in a measure. Alternating, we would have ta-rest-ta-rest to equal one four beat measure. We will stick to this very basic music lesson to play this game.

To play, you will need two sets of drumsticks. These can be purchased relatively cheaply from any music store, or your own can be made using any materials you deem as drumsticks, such as pencils. I found drumsticks and practice pad on www.Amazon.com for $12.99. Then find a place to drum. You might want to stop at a home improvement store and ask for a couple of end pieces of 2x4 instead of drumming on your table. Have two sets available; one for you and one for your student.

Get ready to start. You can start by copying the rhythms provided onto larger pieces of paper that are easy to see and read. Put one set on each piece of paper to begin with. As you progress, you can put multiple rhythms on one piece of paper and start making up your own. Your student may want to make some up at home that you can count out together. Linking several rhythms together can start to make music. Switching them up changes the composition. Varying the strength of the beat changes the feel of the music. This game is easily accomplished by the student and, since it involves rhythm and beat, is liked by most learners.

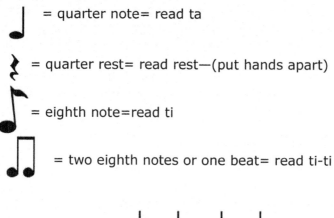

♩ = quarter note= read ta

𝄾 = quarter rest= read rest—(put hands apart)

♪ = eighth note=read ti

♫ = two eighth notes or one beat= read ti-ti

Pattern one   ♩ ♩ ♩ ♩   Read ta-ta-ta-ta

Pattern Two  Read ta-rest-ta-rest

Once you feel comfortable saying the patterns, begin with the drumsticks. Keep saying the beats as you tap them to encourage all the connections that can be made in the brain to be firing. This will encourage the brain to see the notes, process them as music, respond to the visual stimuli with an action. We want the brain to continue to do these steps even after the spoken component is dropped. Here are several more patterns.

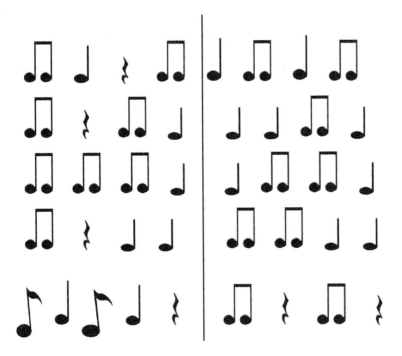

Now make up your own or start putting them together to make new sounds. You can also vary the volume of the strikes and change the speed of the beat to change the feel. Most of all have fun!

185

Letters

The Trials and Tribulation of a Parent

My children's story began in kindergarten when the teacher spoke to me about their inattentiveness within class. Being an educator myself, I had to agree with the teacher but I saw more than just ADD/ADHD. I did follow all the procedures that needed to be in place for my children's success but was never satisfied with the diagnosis of ADHD. I knew that there was something more going on and continued my search for answers.

It was not until the summer of my son's tenth grade year and my daughter's seventh grade year that I finally got the answers that I was looking for. By accident, I was introduced to Auditory Processing Disorder. A parent brought her child's test results into my office and asked me if I could help her with the results and how we could work with her child within our school setting. While going through the results, I started identifying characteristics within my own children. I asked where she had taken her child for tests and once she left my office, I called the institution to set up testing for my children. Within a month my children did have a diagnosis of APD and I began the process of making sure they had what they needed for their success.

It is so difficult to see your children suffer and feel as if they are a failure, call themselves dumb and feel that they will not be able to enter college. Many nights we all cried from the frustration of trying to get through the homework, trying to understand what was discussed within the class and not having all the notes due to not comprehending what all was verbally stated within the class. Through discussions with teachers, some felt that your child was being defiant if they did not answer a question not understanding that they did not process what was just asked of them or they did not hear all that was asked. In an effort to not look stupid in front of their peers they did not ask to have information repeated.

My children have a 504 Plan in place that has helped with their success in school. The plan gives them accommodations and modifications that help ensure they are understanding what is asked of them, they are given copies of notes, etc. This plan has also followed my son into college where he is very successful in college. My children have been blessed to have Mrs. Jennifer Holland as their APD tutor. She has taken the areas that the children struggle in and help improve their functioning. I have seen huge growth in both my children and their self-esteem has soared. Don't get me wrong, they still struggle but they see that they can be successful with a little additional help.

My advice to parents is to learn as much as you can about APD, be a strong advocate for your child and do not let the words "We can't do that" enter into a conversation with your child, teacher or school and use this book, cover to cover, to help your children succeed. I thank God for Mrs. Holland and her work in writing this book.
Linda – Parent of two children with APD

The following letter was composed by Michaela. She is a 16 year old student who has APD. Michaela struggles to pay attention in class and, unlike most other students, does better when she sits at the back of the classroom. Being a social creature, when she is at the front of the classroom, she finds herself looking behind to see what she can attribute the noise she is hearing to. Michaela does have the prosodic presentation although she does not seem to understand what that means to her. Michaela struggles with comprehension and executive function. When given a large assignment, Michaela has a hard time knowing where to start. She does a very good job of asking for help when she needs it now and has learned to color code her notes on note cards to help her remember information. Michaela has aspirations of becoming a doctor and she can do it- as long as she remembers that she is capable, sticks her nose to the grindstone and keeps her goal in mind!

Michaela's Letter:

Dear Reader,

The first thing I have to say is that I am Mrs. Holland's favorite student and she loves me to death!

Living with auditory processing disorder is definitely a challenge. I have always thought that I just had ADD/ADHD, I didn't think there was anything else going on until I was tested for APD.

I remember when I was in about second grade, that some stuff like math wasn't making any sense. It didn't click at all. It still doesn't a lot of the time. I also remember that when I was frustrated, I would just like turn everything off and I was done. I was put on medication when I was in elementary school and things got easier for a while. My grades got better and I could understand. Then I was taken off the medication because I wasn't eating very much and everything got messed up again. My grades went down and I felt stupid. I couldn't understand why my grades went down.

I have always had teachers who would go out of their way to help me and work with me and when they did, even if I didn't like the class, I would work harder. I had one teacher, Mr. Johnson for algebra. Even though I didn't like algebra, he always watched to see if I understood it or not. He always made learning fun for the whole class, but then he would sit down right next to me and go through it step by step or sometimes he would have me bring a chair up next to his desk and go over the work.

I had a physics teacher, Mr. Willenberg who also made class fun and when I got stuck on something, he would go over and explain it in a different way. He was also available before school so I could ask him questions. Sometimes, if he knew I understood a concept, he would have me help explain it to the class. It was nice to feel smart.

I tried the earbud FM system and it drove me crazy. It didn't sound like the teacher's voice was any different. It also brought attention to me that I didn't want. Then in 9th grade, we had classrooms that had the FM system in the smart board. I noticed that everything was clicking and I didn't seem to have any trouble understanding at all. It seemed like it helped all the students, not just me. Then this year, I had one that was supposed to be like a speaker that went in my back pack and it made it sound like the teachers voice was echoing. I didn't use it very long at all.

I notice some things like some times when someone explains things, I have to sit and think about them for a minute. Then sometimes they make sense and sometimes I have to ask questions. I know it takes me a few minutes to process stuff. It sometimes takes me a little longer than my classmates to understand a new concept. I used to think that it meant that I was stupid, now I know that it just means I need more time and that is okay.

I want parents and teachers to know that sometimes we just need a little more time. APD mentally exhausts you by the end of the day. We have to work 10x harder then the other kids to pay attention and concentrate. When we say 'what' again in the classroom, it isn't because we are ignoring our teachers, we are really just trying to keep up and catch what we missed.

For the kids, don't give up on yourself. You can do anything you want to do. Just because something in your brain doesn't work right doesn't mean you can't do it. Just keep trying until you figure it out. And don't be afraid to ask questions.

The next letter is from Rachel. Rachel is a 15 year old girl with APD. Rachel is the tiny thing I refer to in several places in the book. Rachel struggles with short term memory quite a bit. She feels stress from schedule changes and worries about forgetting things she should remember. We work on making plans and short term memory skills. Rachel also discusses what I see as a prosodic presentation here. She struggles with tones, volume and meaning of words; which she describes in her letter. Here is what Rachel wanted the readers to know.

Dear Reader,

My name is Rachel, I am 15 and 1/2 years old and I have APD (Auditory Processing Disorder). I wanted to write this letter to let those of you who have it know how to handle it and those of you who have to "deal" with someone who has it help you understand it a little more. And, how to help them get through all the struggles they will hit and to help them fight APD.

First, I wanted to start with those of you who have APD. You will have to work harder than everyone else and it won't affect just your school work. I am a competitive cheerleader and APD hits that hard too because it is more difficult to memorize counts and remember what the next steps are in new routines. But, after a lot of hard work, struggling, and dedication I don't have as much of a problem as I did back at the beginning. So, the best thing you can do is work hard. Some schools (at least mine) have what we call a 504 plan. It tells your teachers things they should do to help you. You can set it up on your own but one thing that helps INCREDIBLY is an FM System. It is a radio type machine that you hook up to a pair of headphones and the teacher wears an end that has a microphone on it and it goes directly into to your ear and straight to your brain. And, as you read this book, it will explain to you why it should help you.

Next, I wanted to talk to the parents and teachers. First to the parents, sometimes kids with APD can snap at you or talk really rude and they won't mean it. They may not realize that they even said it in a rude way at all. You just have to let them know to watch how they talk to you and let them know, kindly, to be more careful. Your child will also confuse sentences you say up with other things. Sometimes, it can be close and sometimes it can be not even close to what you said. At first, you will think "How did you get that from what I said?" but the more they become helped and the more they learn about it and how to deal with it, the easier it gets for them and if you say "go feed the dog", they won't think you said "Go to bed". They might think you said "Go pet the dog" or "Go let the dog out". Sometimes, we hear one word and we try to put it together by ourselves. Now, teachers, the main thing you have to understand, is that if you talk louder, it won't help. My teachers when they first found out that, they would shout and emphasize random words because they thought it would help, but it didn't. It is also hard, if you have a setup 504 plan and you have the FM system on it, don't announce it in front of everyone. When I had to wear that, I would have to put it in the note section of the 504 that I did NOT what so ever, want them to say anything to anyone or in front of anyone because I was embarrassed, ashamed, and scared of what they might think of me and what rumors they might start, stuff like that. Just remember that we might need some more attention than the other students but don't put us first. Just give us some more individual time and don't get frustrated when we don't understand things at first. Just keep rewording it and simplifying it down so, it's easier for us to understand.

Thank you for reading this. I hope this helps you understand your child, student, or even yourself in what you have just found out about yourself or you've known but you want to learn more. Just don't forget the most important thing for everyone no matter what you are to the APD child even if it's you, don't forget patience. ☺

Glossary

amygdala: the part of the brain considered to be responsible for processing memory and emotional reactions.

auditory processing: What our brains do with what our ears hear.

auditory processing disorder: A level of hearing loss, not related to physical characteristics of hearing causing inconsistencies in an individuals ability to interpret auditory cues. The level of hearing when these factors are present usually begins at a 35% or greater loss. There are 5 types of auditory processing disorder:

1. associative: Involves a slow down in the processing of information when triggers for auditory processing disorder are present, causing the person to feel lost or uncertain of what they have heard.
2. decoding deficit: Involves the inability or a slow down in the ability to incorporate new ideas, words, vocabulary into existing knowledge. The learner does not seem to hear at all when triggers for auditory processing are present.
3. integration: involves difficulty in maintaining focus and control when multiple sensory systems are involved when auditory processing triggers are present.
4. output-organization: involves struggles with executive function and tasks requiring short term memory especially when triggers are present.
5. prosodic: struggle socially as a result of difficulties understanding nuances of language in spoken conversation such as sarcasm. Often have trouble using and understanding the tone of their own and others voices, especially when triggers are present.

brain training: The structured use of cognitive exercises aimed at improving or changing specific areas of neurological function.

cortisol: a steroid hormone produced by the body released in response to stress. Excess cortisol makes it hard to retrieve information from long term memory. High levels also prohibit information from being transferred to long term memory.

comprehension: the ability to understand (reading comprehension: the ability to understand what we read.)

dyscalculia: A term used to describe a learning disability characterized by difficulties with learning and comprehending math, including concepts such as time, money, spatial reasoning and measurement. Those with the disability often struggle to memorize basic math facts.

dysgraphia: A term used to describe a learning disability characterized by difficulty with writing. It can lead to problems with spelling, poor handwriting and difficulty putting thoughts on paper, as well as organizing letters and numbers and keeping track of them on a page. Dysgraphia is linked to both visual and auditory difficulties.

dyslexia: A term used to describe a broad range of disorders that involve difficulty in learning to read or interpret words, letters, and other symbols.

dyspraxia: A term used to describe a learning disability that affects a person's ability to plan and complete fine motor tasks. Those with this condition often have trouble coordinating both fine and gross motor tasks.

executive function: The ability to connect past information with present expectations and to break a task into manageable pieces, make a plan and then follow through with that plan.

extrinsic motivation: refers to behavior resulting in a system of compliance that emphasizes external rewards such as money, fame, grades or other factors outside of the person to motivate behavior and self control.

intrinsic motivation: refers to factors within the person that motivate behavior and determine results. Internal reward system that drives goal related behavior and motivates self control.

learning disability: A neurological condition that inhibits an individuals' ability to store, produce, process or retrieve information. There are three ways the learning is affected.

1. input: the path the information takes into the brain is affected
2. organization: information must be sequenced, abstracted and organized. With learning disabled, the organization often seems to be stored randomly
3. memory: the learners ability to hold onto and retrieve the information when needed is affected

neuroplasticity: refers to changes in neural pathways and synapses which are due to changes in behavior, environment and neural processes, as well as changes resulting from bodily injury. Neuroplasticity explores how the brain changes throughout life and with brain training.

proprioceptive: refers to sensory receptors, found in muscles, tendons, joints, and the inner ear, that detect the motion or position of the body and movement

short term memory: your mental scratch pad for information that needs to be held onto for a minute or less. Typically, there is room for between 5 and 7 pieces of information available in short term memory. It is the information we need to give the brain time to retrieve necessary links to complete a task.

vestibular: Our bodies sense of where it is in space. The vestibular system provides cues for our balance and posture. The vestibular system is made up of 3 fluid filled pouches in the inner ear that work with the sensory input from the ears and eyes and work together to respond to movement and changes in our body directionality and position. The vestibular system works with the bodies proprioceptors to aid in smooth body motions and movements.

visual closure: the abililty to fill in the whole picture when only given incomplete or partial information.

visual discrimination: the ability to understand and process the differences and similarities between shapes, colors, sizes and positions of objects.

visual memory: the ability of the learner to hold details of objects, textures, faces, pictures and words in the mind and recall them when needed.

visual perception: the ability to process and interpret all the information the eye can see

visual tracking: refers to the ability to control the movements of the eyes to follow directed lines of sight without losing our place

working memory: our ability to hold information long enough to work with it. Working memory allows us to mentally perform complex math problems, remember and follow directions to get to a location or keep track of the amount of our purchases at a grocery store. Thought to last five minutes or less, but can be manipulated to continue to perform a task that lasts longer.

Bibliography

Baroody, C. (2009). Early childhood: child, teacher parent. *Online Submission*, Retrieved from http://www.eric.ed.gov/PDFS/ED506777.pdf

Bennet, A., & Bennet, D. (2009). *The human knowledge system: music and brain coherence.* Retrieved from http://www.monroeinstitute.org/journal/the-human-knowledge-system-music-and-brain-coherence

Berkowitz, D. (2004). Stress and students with learning disabilities. Retrieved from http://www.learningassistance.com/2000/Sep00/stress_and_students.htm

Bonnema, T. (2009). Enhancing student learning with brain based learning. *ERIC online submission*, doi: ED510039

Casassanto, D. (1998). *Neuromodulation and neural plasticity.* Unpublished manuscript, Biology, Bryn Mahr College, Retrieved from http://serendip.brynmawr.edu/bb/neuro/neuro98/202s98-paper2/Casasanto2.html

Connell, J. (2009, Fall). The global aspects of brain-based learning. *Educational Horizons*, *88*(1), 28-39. Retrieved from http://www.eric.ed.gov/PDFS/EJ868336.pdf

Duman, B. (2010). The effects of brain-based learning on the academic achievement of students with different learning styles. *Educational practices: Theory and practice*, Retrieved from http://www.eric.ed.gov/PDFS/EJ919873.pdf

Ekred, M, and S Rudin. "Executive Function Deficeits in Children." *ADD-itude Magazine* Spring, 2011: n. pag. Web. 7 Aug 2011. <http://www.additudemag.com/adhd/article/8392.html>.

Editorial Staff. (2009, March 6). *Auditory processing disorder.* Retrieved from http://www.ncld.org/ld- basics/related-issues/information-processing/auditory-processing-disorders-in-detail

Elliot, E, Bhagat, S, & Lynn, S. (2007). Can children with (central) auditory processing disorders ignore irrelevant sounds?. *Research In Developmental Disabilities*, *28*(5), Retrieved from http://proxy.mul.missouri.edu:2159/science?_ob=ArticleURL&_udi=B6VDN-4KJTNG5-2&_user=3419478&_coverDate=11%2F30%2F2007&_rdoc=1&_fmt=high&_orig=search&_origin=search&_sort=d&_docanchor=&view=c&_acct=C000049994&_version=1&_urlVersion=0&_userid=3419478&md5=ab4307d18751a19e1ab2709815350801&searchtype=a

Emanuel, D., Ficca, K., & Korczak, P. (2010). Survey of the diagnosis and treatment of auditory processing disorders. *Ameri-*

can *Journal of Audiology*, *20*, 48=60. Retrieved from http://web.ebscohost.com.proxy.dbrl.org/ehost/pdfviewer/pd fviewer?sid=a3966ecc-1e5d-4c49-86bd-aac1fc6e6597@ses sionmgr114&vid=4&hid=125

Florian, L. (2008). Special or inclusive education: future trends. *British Journal of Special Education*, *35*(4), 202-208. doi: 10.1111/j.1467-8578.2008.00402.x

Fraser, J., Goswami, U., & Conti-Ramsden, G. (2010). Dyslexia and specific language impairment: the role of phonology and auditory processing . *Scientific Studies of Reading*, *14*(1), 8-29. doi: 10.1080/10888430903242068

Hanes DA, McCollum G. *Journal of Vestibular Research* 2006;16(3):75–91. See more at: http://vestibular .org/understanding-vestibular-disorder/human-balance-system#sthash.ag2Q3AoE.dpuf

Katz, J. (1983). Phonemic Synthesis and other auditory skills. In E. Lasky and J. Katz (Eds.), *Central Auditory Processing Disorders: Problems of Speech, Language and Learning*, University Park Press.

Katz, J. (2007). Phonemic Training and Phonemic Synthesis programs. In D. Geffner & D. Ross-Swain (Eds.), *Auditory Processing Disorders: Assessment, Management and Treatment* (255-256). San Diego: Plural Publishing.

Katz, J. & Wilde, L. (1994). Auditory processing disorders. In Katz, J. (Ed). Handbook of clinical audiology. (4th edition.). Baltimore, MD: Williams and Wilkins, (4th ed.). 490-502.

Kraus, N. (2001). Auditory pathway encoding and neural plasticity in children with learning problems. *Audio Neural Otology*, *6*, 221-227. Retrieved from http://www.soc.Northwestern .edu/brainvolts/documents/KrausAudiolNeurootol2001.pdf

Meltzer, L. (2007). Executive function in education: from theory to practice. NewYork, NY: Guilford Press

Moore, D. (2007). Auditory processing disorders: aquisition and treatment. *Journal of Communication Disorders*, *40*(4), Retrieved from http://proxy.mul.missouri.edu:2159/science?_ ob=ArticleURL&_udi=B6T85-4N7XP9M-2&_user=3419478&_ coverDate=08%2F31%2F2007&_rdoc=1&_fmt= high&_orig= search&_origin=search&_sort=d&_docanchor=&view=c&_acc t=C000049994&_version=1&_urlVersion=0&_userid=341947 8&md5=fe9a2c74b490675ce8e574f2816a72d7&searchtype= a

Potts, B. (1993). improving the quality of students notes. *Practical Assessment, Research and Evalutaion*, Retrieved from http://pareonline.net/getvn.asp?v=3&n=8 doi: 1531-7714

Quily, P. (October 2010). Adhd children have nearly 4 x risk for depression and suicide attempts and depression [Web log message]. Retrieved from http://adultaddstrengths.com/20 10/10/06/adhd-children-have-nearly-4-times-higher-risk-for-suicide-attempts-and-depression/

Ray, L. (2009, October). Speech exercises for stroke victims. Retrieved from http://www.livestrong.com/article/19483-speech -exercises-stroke-victims/

Ross-Swain, D. (2007). The effects of auditory stimulation on auditory processing disorder: a summary of the findings. International Journal of Listening, 21(2), Retrieved from http://proxy.mul.missouri.edu:11809/ids70/view_record.php ?id=2&recnum=9&log=from_res&SID=j0dr5nrmrqqetcijr54vd g0m51&mark_id=search%3A2%3A0%2C0%2C10

Scharer, P. (October 2004). Is it auditory processing disorder or add?. ADDitude: Living Well with Attention deficit disorder, Retrieved from http://www.additudemag.com/adhd/article/ 731.html

Scull, J., & Winkler, A. (2011). Shifting trends in special education. *Thomas B Fordham Institute*, Retrieved from http:// www.eric.ed.gov/PDFS/ED520416.pdf

Shumway-Cook A, Woollacott MH. *Motor Control: Theory and Practical Applications.* Philadelphia: Lippincott, Williams & Wilkins; 2001.

University of Michigan (2008, May 5). Brain-training To Improve Memory Boosts Fluid Intelligence. *ScienceDaily*. Retrieved December 4, 2011, from http://www.sciencedaily.com- /releases/2008/05/080505075642.htm

Wallachl, G. (2011). Peeling the onion of auditory processing dosorder: a language/curricular perspective. *Language, Speech and Hearing services in Schools*, 42, 273-285. Retrieved from http://web.ebscohost.com.proxy.dbrl.org/ehost/detail?vid=4 &hid=125&sid=a3966ecc-1e5d-4c49-86bd-aac1fc6e6597@ sessionmgr114&bdata=JnNpdGU9ZWhvc3QtbGl2ZQ==

"What Teachers Should Know and Be Able to Do." *www.nbpts.org*. National Board for Professional Teaching Standards, 08/2002. Web. 6 Aug 2011. http://www.nbpts .org/ UserFiles/File/what_teachers.pdf.

Wilmes, B. (2008). Coming to our senses: incorporating brain research findings into classroom insturction. Retrieved from http:// search.ebscohost.com.proxy.dbrl.org/login.aspx?direct=true&db =tfh&AN=32708998&site=ehost-live

Willis, J. (2006). *Research based strategies to ignite student learning*. Alexandria, VA: ASCD

CPSIA information can be obtained
at www.ICGtesting.com
Printed in the USA
BVOW09s0711280617
488021BV00008B/200/P